Escape from the Trap of Tradition

Helping Pastors and Believers Transition Out of Tradition

Understanding For Life
Ministries, Inc.
3665 Kirby Pkwy., Suite 6
Memphis, TN 38115
(901) 844-3962

ALTON R. WILLIAMS
FOREWORD BY APOSTLE JOHN ECKHARDT

Unless otherwise indicated, all Scripture quotations are taken from the *King James Version* of the Bible.

My Escape From The Trap of Tradition

ISBN 0-9721504-3-9
Copyright © 2003 Apostle Alton R. Williams
All rights reserved

PUBLISHED BY

Understanding For Life Ministries, Inc.
3665 Kirby Parkway
Suite 6
Memphis, TN 38115

2003
First Edition

Printed in the United States of America.

All rights reserved under International Copyright Law.
Contents and/or cover may not be reproduced in whole or in part in any form without the expressed written consent of the Publisher.

DEDICATION

This book is dedicated first of all to my Lord and Savior, Jesus Christ, who chooses, leads, guides, anoints and releases His grace and giftings for our lives and ministries. I thank Him for seeing fit to place me in the ministry even when I wanted no part of it. Your long suffering is so amazing. I thank Him for His love and patience when I tried to run from every calling He has ever placed upon me. I have found the Word to be true when it says *"the giftings and callings of God are without repentance" (Romans 11:29).*

To my precious wife, Sherrilyn, whose love, affection and support never ceases to amaze me. You are one of God's most honored and cherished vessels for today. The anointing of God is definitely on your life. Thank you for being my "sideline coach" who continues to work to see me reach my fullest potential. That gift of encouragement and motivation you have is simply awesome. You are truly a helpmeet from Heaven. Your book served as an inspiration for me to finish this project. You told me six years ago that I needed to do this book. Your love and push has made this a reality. When God was changing my course in ministry 16 years ago, it was your faith and trust in me that was key to us being where we are today. Thank you my Sanguine love.

To my five precious children: Altronise, Sheronda, Alton Jr., Allison and Joy. I have not overlooked the sacrifices of Daddy's time that you have had to make. When I had to be at church at times when I probably should have been at home; when I had to take long prayer excursions; when Daddy had to study and could not spend the adequate time I needed to spend with you, you continued to love and understand me. I look forward to seeing who God has destined you to be and us working together in ministry.

To the memory of my father and mother, the late Rev. & Mrs. Jasper W. Williams, Sr., whose blood, sweat and tears went into loving, providing and caring for me. I was probably the sickest of any of the four children. They went through great sacrifice in rearing me because of polio and constant battles with pneumonia and asthma. I would not be here were it not for the love of my mother. I can see her now going through the cold, heat, sleet, snow, and rain to carry me to doctors, hospitals and buying medication so that I would be here to fulfill my destiny in God. Thank you Momma.

My father saw in me what I did not see in myself. He tried so hard to get me to become close to him so that he could train me for the ministry. Yet, he lovingly accepted my constant rejections when I wanted to go contrary to God's plan for my life. It was because of your labor in God's vineyard that I am where I am today. Thank you, Daddy for the preaching legacy that you left this family for generations to come and for leaving me a track record of honesty and integrity. You left a church with a great spiritual foundation. Because of your work, I took over a church that was debt free with finances in the bank. You shall never be forgotten.

To my brother Jasper, who became almost like a father to me. By the time I came into the ministry, Daddy was not of mental capacity where he could help mentor me. That responsibility fell to you, my brother. Thank you for all of the wisdom and ministry advice you have given me to help me come to where I am today. Your ministry has made a lasting impact on my life.

To my sister, Nealey, who growing up I was probably closer to than anyone else in the family. You gave me self-confidence when I didn't have any because of my handicap. Although we went through a lot of struggles in our later adult years, I praise God that He has restored that closeness and that I can still call you my sister and that you are a part of my life and ministry.

To my sister Janice, who was somewhat the loner or outsider to all of the family church struggles. We had our sibling rivalries growing up, but I thank God for the love and closeness we share now. When you can match friendship with a blood sister, you have an awesome combination. I'm so glad you missed the fireworks (smile).

To my Administrative Assistant, Sandra Cox, who outside of my wife and family knows me better than anyone else in the church. You have the distinction of working with me longer than any other staff person. Thank you for your labor in typesetting this work and making it a reality. I know you've got to be tired! (smile)

To my staff elders and church staff. Thank you for bearing the load to give me time to get alone with God and write this book. Your work helps to make your pastor look good. I love you all.

To my church, World Overcomers Outreach Ministries Church. Thank you for your submission and obedience in allowing me to lead and pastor you. A pastor is not your pastor unless you allow him to pastor you and you have done that. I would not want to pastor any other people. God has married us and unless He changes the assignment, I promise you there will be no divorce. Let's run with the vision and reel in the harvest for Jesus. Your love and patience has been key in my transition from a pastoral anointing to an apostolic anointing.

To the members of old Lane Avenue Baptist Church, many of whom are still with me today. I know the many transitions out of tradition were not easy. I know there were many decisions and changes made that you did not understand, but praise God you stuck with me. It was upon your foundation that this new move of God as World Overcomers Outreach Ministries Church was built upon. We see in the news everyday how many churches resist change and the truth of God's Word and have split apart. Although our church experienced a separation over 12 years ago, it was not because of your rejection of the truth. I love you.

I also dedicate this book to the part of the Lane Avenue Baptist Church family who departed in the separation before I ever came back to Memphis. These members, with the exception of a few, ultimately evolved into the Christ Baptist Church, pastored by Rev. James A. Williams, who once served as one of my deacons. You all will always be a part of me. Your work and sacrifice in the building of Lane Avenue will never be forgotten.

Finally, I would like to dedicate this book and honor the ministry of Apostle John Eckhardt, whose books and teachings have mentored me into this new apostolic reformation movement. Thank you for pioneering the revelation of the apostle's gift back to the Body of Christ. Because of you I have found out who I am.

Table of Contents

Foreword
Introduction 1

Chapter 1 "My Beginnings" 5
Chapter 2 "Getting Out of
            Tradition's Boat" 11

Chapter 3 "Defining Tradition" 27
Chapter 4 "Traditions Of The Church" 35

Chapter 5 "Finding What God Has
            Prepared For You" 47

Chapter 6 "If You Can Give It Up,
            You Can Have It All" 55

Chapter 7 "The School of Family" 73
Chapter 8 "Going And Not Knowing" 89

Chapter 9 "You Must Deal With
            Persecution" 97

Chapter 10 "Walking By Faith" 103

Chapter 11 "God's Phone Call For
            Me To Return" 109

Chapter 12 "The Beginning of the Church's
            Transformation" 117

Chapter 13	"The Hundredfold Manifestation"	125
Chapter 14	"The Test For Pastors"	143
Chapter 15	"Tradition And The Word Movement"	147
Chapter 16	"Destiny Found"	173
Bibliography		177

FOREWORD

We are living in a time of great transition and change. This is happening both naturally and spiritually. The church is presently enjoying a new reformation. These are glorious and challenging days to be a believer.

Those who are sensitive to the voice of the Holy Spirit are following the cloud of His glory and open to change. One such person is Alton Williams. You are holding in your hand a book that contains a powerful testimony of the blessings of overcoming tradition and moving into the present truth.

Progress and advancement necessitate change. Many are resistant to change because of tradition. Tradition has always been a major hindrance for many in times of transition and change.

Tradition has the power to make the commandments of God of none effect *(Matthew 15:6)*. This is why overcoming tradition is a major breakthrough for any leader or believer. This is also why I highly recommend this book. I have seen Alton Williams move with the Holy Spirit and follow the cloud. I have seen the results of boldness and courage to change. This has resulted in a radical paradigm shift in his message and ministry.

Much of what Alton Williams has done has been **PIONEERING**. This is a testimony of the apostolic grace that is upon his life and ministry. Apostles pioneer new paths and ways for others to follow. This book will encourage other leaders to rise up and follow through to victory.

I believe there are many leaders and believers who will read this book and be challenged to move from tradition into present truth. Overcoming tradition may be the greatest battle you will ever face. The testimony in this book will help you overcome the insidious trap of tradition and help thrust you forward into your destiny. Don't allow tradition to hold you back. Rise up and move forward in your destiny and be inspired by others, like Alton Williams, who have already succeeded.

—Apostle John Eckhardt
Crusaders Ministries
Chicago, IL

INTRODUCTION

MILLIONS DIDN'T MAKE IT, BUT I WAS ONE OF THE ONES WHO DID

In the year 2000, I received God's call to walk in the ministry gift of the Apostle. There is much misunderstanding in the Body of Christ concerning this office. One of the main functions of this gifting is to bring reform to the church. The church is experiencing reformation right now, which means God is working change in His people; changes that will affect every area of our lives, particularly in our mindsets and in the way we think. Tradition is a mindset, a stronghold established by a religious spirit.

God uses apostles to boldly challenge the status quo and force change for the better. They are sent by God to correct things that are not in line with God's purpose for His church. Whenever there is need for reformation, the Lord sends forth apostles. Apostles have the ability to pull down the strongholds of tradition and bring forth new revelation.

Man's religious systems that have been set up for years are the greatest enemies to a new move of God. Religious systems that do need reform serve the interests of the leadership of that system. When their power, prestige, position, and control over God's people are at stake, they will become offended at truth and will fight to hold on to their beliefs. They will do whatever they can to resist a reformation.

Apostles are called upon to be bold by confronting and correcting man's religious traditions that hinder people from walking according to the truth. Apostles take a stand for truth and defend it. Their major concern is that the church continues in truth.

The truth of God's Word and the truth of the Gospel must be defended. The Gospel is the good news that Jesus saves from sin, sickness, poverty, depression, curses, demons and hell. It is a "full gospel" of deliverance from all results of

Adam's transgression. It is for this reason that we write this book. The spirit of tradition has forsaken these things and the people of God must be informed.

This book is for the Christian who desires to come out but doesn't know how. It is also for the pastor who wants to see transformation in his church but is afraid. It's time, like Peter, to step out of the boat and walk on the water.

It is my prayer that this book is not perceived to be a "bashing" of any church denomination. I believe that any church that upholds the doctrines and traditions of the scriptures as given by the apostles, especially as it pertains to the doctrines of Christ, is a church of the Lord Jesus Christ *(2 John 9-10)*.

Most of us were saved in a traditional or denominational church. We thank God that we found the Lord there and received our early foundational knowledge of Him in those churches. We thank God for the pastors who taught us values and taught us principles of the scriptures to live by. It is our intent, however, to expose the **SPIRIT OF TRADITION AND RELIGION** designed to hinder the church from knowing its God and finding its purpose. Religion has been exalted above the Word of God and it hinders the Word from affecting our lives. Without the knowledge and truth of God's Word, we cannot effectively know or walk with God, which means we can never know His ways and ultimately never find His purpose and destiny for our lives.

God does not hate or dislike any Christian denomination. However, when the teachings of any church or organization are inconsistent with the Word and cause people to deviate from knowing the Father and having a deeper relationship with Him, those traditions must be exposed. Yet, there are many men of God who are making transformations right within their denominations. There are many Spirit-filled Baptists, Methodists, Catholics, etc.

The Word of God lets us know that all traditions are not bad:

*"Whereunto he called you by our gospel, to the obtaining of the glory of our Lord Jesus Christ. Therefore, brethren, **STAND FAST, AND HOLD THE TRADITIONS WHICH YE HAVE BEEN TAUGHT, WHETHER BY WORD, OR OUR EPISTLE.**"*

(2 Thessalonians 2:14-15)

Paul admonished us to hold to those traditions that he taught through the Word or his epistles. Many church and denominational traditions have omitted many of the traditions that the apostle's epistles taught, which also weakens the impact of God's Word. It's like a doctor who gives you a prescription for some medication that requires three different ingredients in order for it to have the power to do the job. The pharmacist, out of ignorance, only uses two ingredients. The medication will not have the necessary impact to cure the illness. The same is true spiritually when we accept only part of the Word. For example, if we preach a salvation of only easy mental believing without repentance of heart, it will not produce true salvation and change.

People are looking for more than religion. They don't always know what they are looking for, but they know that it is something more to God than what they experience each Sunday morning. They don't want to be proselyted into another denomination. They are tired of being fitted into another doctrinal mold that someone may gloat over them as converts. They want something that is bigger and higher than all denominational groups. They want to know God and see His power that will enable them to effectively reach the lost, doomed and dying before it is too late.

The traditions of men will rob you of seeing the supernatural power of God, answered prayer, faith, healing, authority over Satan and his kingdom, deliverance, victory, peace of mind, miracles, prosperity, the blessings of God, your inheritance and your assignment for life.

Today there are many in the church of the Lord Jesus Christ who are struggling to be free from the chains and shackles of tradition. The lost need to be saved, the sick need to be healed, the empty need to be filled and those who are oppressed and possessed of the devil need to be delivered.

We do not have much time. The harvest is waiting to be gathered. To do this work, we must have the power of the Holy Ghost. Just as God used Moses to deliver Israel, He has called many deliverers for His people. No doubt, if you are reading this book, you are one of them.

God is seeking to reach all of His deliverers by setting a bush aflame of His power and glory within them. I pray that this book will help to light the fire of your spirit.

Through **MY ESCAPE FROM THE TRAP OF TRADITION**, I pray that it ministers a testimony to you, that if "I" can come out of it, anyone who has the heart and desire can come out also.

That's why I'm proud to say, "**MILLIONS DIDN'T MAKE IT, BUT I WAS ONE OF THE ONES WHO DID!** So can you.

1

MY BEGINNINGS

On December 11, 1953, I was born into a family of Baptist preachers. My father, uncle, and brother were all well known by the time I was a teenager. My brother, who was ten years older than me, was pastoring a growing, thriving church in Atlanta, Georgia and was traveling all over the country running revivals. The last thing I wanted to do was preach, because I knew coming behind all of those footsteps, I would never have a chance. People would never give me a chance to be me and would always make comparisons.

At 19 months of age, I contracted polio in my right leg. I wore braces and high top shoes, and as a result I experienced great ridicule and rejection from friends and peers. I had several major bouts with pneumonia during my early elementary school years and probably should have died. I suffered with asthma, allergies and hay fever. My family sheltered me from a lot because of these illnesses, and my father was very over-protective of me. He even bought a rental house that he wanted to reserve for my future. In the event polio limited my activities in life, I could have my own store to make a living. He was a man of great love, compassion and foresight. All of these things however, contributed to me growing up and battling with low self-esteem.

At age 11, I accepted the Lord as my Savior with hesitancy. For four nights I would not accept the Lord simply because of how my father posed the question to me each night. He asked four nights in a row, "A. R., do you feel anything?" My response each night was, "No." I was only being honest. I would check myself inside to see if I felt anything or had any kind of special feelings. Nope, didn't feel a thing. I didn't know it at the time, but that was one of the church's traditions – salvation based on feelings. You had to feel something, sense something or see something in order to prove you were saved. This ultimately led many people to fabricate an experience just to prove that they were saved.

After four nights of my father being frustrated and embarrassed by his son's refusal to accept Christ, finally on that Friday night, he changed his question and asked,

"A. R., can you believe in Jesus?" When he said that, I immediately got up from what was called the "mourners' bench" went to the chairs seated in front for those who accepted the Lord. Yes, I could believe. Daddy finally asked it according to how the scriptures presented it, by faith or belief and not by feelings (Romans 10:9).

Looking back on it, these were some of the beginning manifestations of my apostolic nature. Apostles are defenders of truth and they despise the traditions and commandments of men. My apostolic nature was refuting my own father.

As I grew into my teen years, my father constantly pursued me to accept my call into the ministry. He shared with me many times how he knew the Lord had called me to preach and how I would one day be the pastor of Lane Avenue. I would find reasons to avoid being around him because I knew that's what he was going to talk about. At that time, I was too into my R & B music. All I wanted to do was become a radio DJ, spin records at dances and become a high school principal.

I was running from God's call on my life. Deep down I knew that my father was right. Yet, I despised him somewhat for pressuring me to preach. That was part of my reason for running. I wanted to show him that he could not force me to preach. That was why I wanted to do that which was contrary to that of a preacher and spin records.

Growing up in a preacher's home, you want to see and enjoy the world. Had my father left me alone and not tried to persuade me to preach, I probably would have come around much sooner. He saw in me what I could not see in myself. My father also knew that he was getting older and was going to need some help that he could trust in the pulpit. He never trusted my brother-in-law (my sister's first husband). He always felt and inwardly knew that all my brother-in-law wanted was the church when he died. He expressed this to my brother and me many times. Of course, he could never tell my sister that because of his love for her and that was her husband.

I taught high school from 1977 to 1981 and was preparing to apply for an assistant principal position. You had to have taught in the school system for three years with a Master's Degree in Educational Administration and Supervision, which I received in August of 1980. I was ready to be a high school principal. However, something funny happened on the way to my "principalship".

On a Sunday night in August of 1979, I went to hear the first sermon of a good friend of mine. That night I saw myself preaching as he preached. I was impressed with how young but boldly he preached. From that night on, until the next day, I cried with conviction. Monday morning during my free period as a teacher at Germantown High School, I told God that if He let me finish this last semester of my Master's Degree work, I would accept my call and confess it to the church the Sunday after my last class, which was the 2nd Sunday in December of that year. I preached my first sermon in January 1980.

On January 12, 1981, my father went home to be with the Lord. Now the pressure was on. Everybody knew my brother was not coming back to pastor the church because he was too well established in Atlanta. All eyes were now on me. I was now the family's hope and standard-bearer.

Prior to my father's death, I tried my best to run from this calling. I quit coming to church for a while because I wanted to be nowhere near anything that concerned preaching. Yet, I will never forget when the church dedicated its new fellowship hall in May of 1980. Daddy was sick and was unable to preach during this particular period. The deacons asked me to dedicate the building in place of my father. I had been preaching for about four months and was running from being the next pastor. We all knew Daddy did not have long.

While standing at the door cutting the ribbon to dedicate the "J. W. Williams Fellowship Hall", something came all over me that God was calling me to pastor the church. I kept running because the last thing I wanted to do was pastor folk I grew up knowing, many of whom put diapers on me. However, while at the door cutting the ribbon, that's when I knew it.

Finally, election night July 1981, my name was put in nomination for pastorate against my brother-in-law. He married my oldest sister in 1967 and had served as my father's pulpit assistant for 14 years up until his death. At this time however, he had pulled away from my sister and was in the process of divorcing her. He had begun talking to other members in the church and was now confident that he could win the election without the family's attachment.

My brother officiated the election that night. I wouldn't even attend. I was not there to even vote for myself. I was inwardly hoping that I would not win. I won by about 100 votes. Most of the people who voted against me were people who were made promises of position in the church by my brother-in-law and saw themselves as having a better chance to lead and be exalted in church than under a "Williams" regime.

Others who had also voted for my brother-in-law told me later that they felt I would be ruled and controlled by my family, and that's why they wouldn't vote for me.

Now I was pastor. I felt like I had the weight of the world on my shoulders. Deep down I never felt like it was mine. I always felt the vote might have been different had it not been for the presence of my brother and mother. A lot of people probably would have voted the other way and those that voted for me either wanted to keep my mother in control or they just knew which way the wind was going to blow and was smart enough to vote for me. They could not have been voting for me, I had no experience at the time. As a matter of fact, I had preached only three sermons by this time.

I spent the first six years of my ministry trying to find myself as a preacher. As the son and brother of well-known preachers, I received many invitations to preach at local churches in the city. There were a few occasions when I went out of town to preach. There was one in particular that I remember quite well. A pastor in Chicago, Illinois, who was a good friend of my brother, called me to preach at his Men's Day Celebration. Before going, I begged him not to tell his people who my brother was. Chicago was one of my brother's best cities to preach in. He was very well known there. I had been preaching about two years, and I knew if they knew who my brother was, I would never have a chance. Sure enough he did just the opposite and told them I was Jasper Williams' brother. He knew it would build his crowd if he told them that.

Boy, I fell on my face and died three deaths in that pulpit. I tried to preach like my brother because that's what they wanted. People were comparing. They were cold as ice. Yet it was my fault. I had not learned how to trust the Holy Ghost. I was trusting in my own strengths and abilities. I learned a great lesson that day. God made only one Jasper Williams, Sr. and one Jasper Williams, Jr. You have got to be yourself or rather who God has made you to be.

I used to hear my brother tell me how he started preaching at age 6 and traveled with my father preaching as a little boy. They were very close and he received hands-on training from my dad. I used to hate that I was not extended this privilege. I didn't start preaching until I was 26 years old. I had no knowledge and no experience, but was thrust into the pastorate my father had founded.

Looking back on it, however, had I been brought up and trained under my father, it would have been more difficult for me to move in the direction God had prepared for me. I missed having many of the Baptist preacher traditions engrafted in me. Once a preacher is indoctrinated or proselytized into a particular theological tradition, it is difficult to escape. Although I grew up in a preacher's home, I had no interest in it growing up. It was not until I was about to confess my call into the ministry that I started seeing the need to learn more about God, theology and the Bible. So I missed that indoctrination.

What a lot of people don't know is that pastors and preachers, in many cases, are more spiritually bound than the people they preach to. Why? Because schools and peers in the ministry tend to teach preachers what they should preach and what they should believe. Their preacher ego and image is now at stake. Their reputation as "one of the boys" is at stake. The people in the pews don't have that pressure and are many times less inhibited to receive from God. I saw members in the early days blessed, healed, and receive answers to prayers, and I couldn't because of my indoctrination into unbelief by preachers and seminaries (Matthew 23:15).

Therefore, by the time I found out about the Holy Ghost Baptism, even though I had a few hang-ups that I learned from my Baptist background and in seminary, my heart opened to it a little sooner. Had I been grounded in my denominational traditions as a child, it would have not been impossible, but more difficult to make the transition to truth.

2
GETTING OUT OF TRADITION'S BOAT

The following account is the beginning of my escape out of tradition. Everything starts with the Baptism with the Holy Ghost. There has been so much misunderstanding about it. I pray that my experience and testimony can bring many more of God's hungry children into that place of full joy and victory.

Satan uses fear, misunderstanding, debate and confusion on this subject to keep people from entering in, because he knows that you will receive a greater potential of defeating him in your personal life and ministry. I sought to serve the Lord with my full being in the first six years of my ministry, but always found myself limited by something I could not put my finger on. I used to think the problem was external; maybe I needed another church with new members or maybe I needed to institute some new programs in the church! No, the problem was not outside but inside. I was lacking something. The Lord had to show me that in order to serve Him fully and completely, I had to have power. My traditions told me that I had all that God had to give when I received Christ as my Savior, but I found that was untrue. I believed that because that was what I was told to believe.

All the preachers, scholars, commentaries, leading Bible authorities and mainline denominations taught this. Well, the Bible teaches differently and I'm glad I found that out. Believe me, my fellow Christians and pastors, the Baptism of the Holy Ghost is real. You can argue and debate forever, but experience will kill all arguments. This is my story. I hope you may also come to know Jesus not only as Savior and Lord, but also as Baptizer with the Holy Spirit. In order to do it, you must be like Peter and make the decision to get out of the boat. Peter was willing to leave his fellow disciples in the boat while in that storm and walk on water *(Matthew 14:29)*. Only "water walkers" can come out of tradition. I'm sure Peter's fellow disciples probably thought he was crazy and attempted to coerce him back into the boat. Your fellow peers will try to do you the same way. "You can't do that. That's not normal. Get back in the boat. Play it safe. Stay like us, because what you're doing is not Baptist, Methodist, COGIC (Church of God In Christ), Presbyterian or Lutheran." In other words, stay mediocre like us.

Although, the Baptism with the Holy Ghost, with the evidence of speaking in other tongues was never discussed in my family of Baptist preachers, it was not consistent with our denomination's theology. If you were to bring that subject up to us, we would have probably responded as the Ephesian believers did when approached by Paul about it:

*"We have not so much as heard whether there be any **HOLY GHOST**."*
(Acts 19:2)

Of course, as Baptists, we knew that the Holy Spirit came in to dwell when we accepted Jesus as Lord and Savior to produce the life of Christ in us *(Romans 8:9)*. The Holy Spirit, however, was never presented as a separate person of the Godhead assigned to bring us power.

*"But **YE SHALL RECEIVE POWER**, after that the **HOLY GHOST IS COME UPON YOU**: and ye shall be witnesses unto me both in Jerusalem, and in all Judea, and in Samaria and unto the uttermost part of the earth."*
(Acts 1:8)

We knew the Holy Ghost came in us, but we were never taught that He came **UPON** us. The only baptism we knew about was in water and in the body of Christ *(1 Corinthians 12:13)*, but we were never taught that we could be baptized in the Holy Ghost and with fire *(Matthew 3:11; Acts 1:5)*. In fact, our tradition taught us that it was the same experience as being baptized in the Body. I never knew that these were two separate experiences, since we had traditionally seen all three persons of the Godhead as the same person.

As a young adult, I heard how COGIC talked about having the Holy Ghost. I saw that their style of worship was different from ours. My father used to preach for the Presiding Bishop at that time, Bishop J. O. Patterson, Sr.

My second orientation to the Holy Ghost came through my wife's mother, who was the pastor of a Pentecostal Holiness Church. During the time I was courting and pursuing my wife, there were many nights I had to attend church with them. I saw them dance, run, speak in tongues, pray all night, lay hands on the sick and cast out devils. But due to, the strict holiness doctrinal teachings of the church, I was turned off and wanted no part of it. Yet, I knew they had something that I did not have.

The crowning moment for me that began my quest was in 1986 on a trip with my wife to Charlotte, NC. We would vacation at the old PTL Heritage USA Campgrounds and Resort founded by Jim Bakker. It was one of the greatest places on the face of this earth for a Christian to rest and relax.

We attended a TV taping one day and at the conclusion of the show, the Holy Spirit manifested and an impromptu service took place. As the people lifted their hands and worshipped, the place became eerily silent. All of a sudden, someone at the top of the TV studio auditorium began speaking in a strange unknown language. Shortly afterwards, someone else from clear over on the other side of the studio gave an interpretive message in English in response to the one in tongues. It was so awesome and so beautiful. I had never witnessed or experienced a service like that before. I left that service with renewed passion and vision. I knew I had to have what they had. I began thinking that maybe this was what I was looking for.

We had friends who were employed by PTL at the time, Russ and Sandy Hosey. I knew Sandy from our college days at LeMoyne-Owen College. We saw them one day, and they invited us to their home for dinner. I explained to them what I was looking for and how I wanted to receive this experience. They ministered to me but nothing happened. They told me that sometimes when you have had a lot of traditional teachings taught to you, the faith to receive is hindered. Sometimes you have to unlearn old things before you can learn new things.

By this time, I had been around other preachers who spoke against this kind of teaching. Books and Sunday school quarterlies that I read taught against it. Bible commentaries wrote that it was not for today. The seminary I attended was also not a proponent of this doctrine. By now as a pastor, I had been religiously indoctrinated.

The Hoseys told me that there are usually one of two reasons why people cannot or have a hard time receiving the Holy Ghost: 1) a lack of faith or 2) a lack of yieldedness. It was both for me. They encouraged me to read books that would build my faith first and wash out unbelieving doctrines, which taught that tongues went out with the apostles, and are no longer needed.

When I returned home, I slowly began losing my hunger for receiving and returned to my routine of doing religious works. Yet, something was missing and was not right. There was still a constant, nagging sensation within me that I was incomplete and needed more.

I saw my members' lives being destroyed and I had nothing to offer to help them. I saw many of them dying young before it was their time to go, and all I could do was pray, "Lord if it be thy will, heal them or let them live" *(Ecclesiastes 7:17)*. I couldn't pray in faith because I did not know His will. I had to find out that His Word was His will, and His will was whatever He promised in His Word *(1 John 5:14)*.

I later had a member to challenge me about speaking in tongues (I will tell this story in a later chapter). My people's eyes were opening, and I had better hurry up and get this thing finalized in my life.

But what would my brother think? What would fellow pastors in the city think? What would my members think? Yet, the questions in my mind did not have the power to quench the thirst and hunger that was now in my heart. I knew that there was something more, and God knew that I knew and He was holding me accountable.

God placed pastors in my path who prayed for me to receive and nothing happened. I had people who ministered to me who were praying in the most beautiful language. They had a rhythmic, fluent expression of tongues. They laid hands on me and told me to continue speaking. I started saying in my mind, "What do you mean?" "Say what?" The only thing that came out of my mouth was noise that you would make at the doctor's office when he puts the stick down your throat, Aa-ah! Sometimes I wouldn't say anything because I waited for something to overtake me and make me speak, meaning that I would not yield.

I remember somewhere around the third or fourth time I was ministered to by someone, tears were streaming down my face. By now I was tired of the frustration and the disappointment. I remember going to services that gave an invitation to receive the Holy Spirit. They would call you to come down. I remember saying to myself, "I can't walk down that aisle. I can't let people see this Baptist pastor coming down the aisle to speak in tongues." I wanted it, but I wanted to receive in private. I was like "**NICK AT NITE.**" Nicodemus went in the night to pursue Jesus. He knew Jesus had something that he needed, but he couldn't go to Him in front of his peers. He had too much to lose *(John 3:1-2)*.

My pride would not allow me to receive openly. I was afraid of how I would look in front of others. Would I look stupid? In reality I was still ashamed of being associated with this or ashamed of what Jesus' own Word had declared.

15

*"For whosoever shall be **ASHAMED OF ME AND OF MY WORDS**, of him shall the Son of man be ashamed..."*

(Luke 9:26)

I would wait until the invitation was over and the converts or people who had responded were going down the aisle to the prayer room, then I would sneak to the prayer room after they got upstairs. Again, I left feeling rejected by God.

This lasted for almost a year. In April of 1987, I set out to obey another inner nagging in my soul – go to Tulsa to attend Rhema Bible Training Center. I had read Kenneth Hagin's books and had received the simplicity of the Gospel message that he taught. My daughter was going through a great physical affliction and his books taught me that healing was available to me and my children (I will also elaborate more on this in a later chapter).

Finally, that April, I had a chance to do some intense reading while spending a week in Tulsa. I laid on the bed in my hotel room and read Fred Price's book **_The Holy Spirit, The Missing Ingredient_**. As I read his account of how he sought the Baptism with the Holy Ghost and became frustrated, tears streamed down my face. It blessed me because I thought something was wrong with me and therefore, God had reason to reject me. When I saw that he experienced the same thing, I knew there was still hope for me.

I went from that to reading **_This Awakening Generation_** by John Osteen, a Baptist pastor who had a sick daughter that wanted more of God's power. I stayed up all night shedding tears while reading each page. I knew without a doubt God was leading me. I felt I was reading my own story. God used these two books to almost answer every question and doubt that I had. Yet, deep down I still had some hindering questions.

I was still afraid of speaking in tongues, because I was told that it was of the devil and that I might pray for the

Holy Ghost and get a demon. Satan has strategically placed fear and doubt in the minds of thousands of believers to keep us from this experience. One of the books answered this question by using *Luke 11:11-13*:

> *"If a son shall ask bread of any of you that is a father, will he give him a stone? Or if he ask a fish,* **WILL HE FOR A FISH GIVE A SERPENT?** *Or if he shall ask an egg,* **WILL HE OFFER HIM A SCORPION?** *If ye then, being evil, know how to give good gifts unto your children:* **HOW MUCH MORE SHALL YOUR HEAVENLY FATHER GIVE THE HOLY SPIRIT TO THEM THAT ASK HIM?**

 I knew God was saying to me that if I prayed to the Father for something, He would not give me something evil or something other than what I asked. The serpent and scorpion symbolize the devil and demons (*Luke 10:19*).

 Verse 13 also revealed something that blew my theology out of the water. We were never taught to ask for the Holy Spirit. We were taught at salvation to ask God to save us and receive Jesus, but this passage says that we can ask the Father to give us the Holy Spirit (as if we didn't already have Him). "Father" indicates the person is already saved, or otherwise we cannot refer to God as our "Heavenly Father." Yet, we are to ask for the Holy Ghost. This told me that the Holy Ghost was a subsequent experience to salvation. **GOD'S GIFT TO THE WORLD IS JESUS. HIS GIFT TO THE BELIEVER OR THE CHURCH IS THE HOLY GHOST.**

 My next doubt was whether or not tongues were still for today and had not gone away with the death of the apostles. *1 Corinthians 13:8* tells us that tongues and the other gifts would one day vanish and cease. However, this will not occur until that which is perfect is come (man's perfect state of being), which will not happen until we get to

Heaven (*verse 10*). That will also be the day that we stand before the Lord face to face (*verse 12*). That means tongues are here to stay until we all stand before the Lord face to face.

I discovered that scripture taught that people were receiving the Holy Spirit days after salvation. Based upon how we as Baptist believed, once you were saved, the Holy Ghost came in at that moment, and you had all the experience of the Holy Ghost you would ever need. This was a key area where tradition had my mind bound. I looked up each scripture, however, in my own Bible as given by the books I had read and saw that what these men wrote was true.

1. Paul was saved on the Damascus Road when he called on the Lord *(Acts 9:6; Romans 10:13)*. However, three days later he received the Holy Ghost *(Acts 9:9,17)*.

2. The Disciples had already received the indwelling of the Holy Ghost for the forgiveness of sin in *John 20:22-23*. Yet, 40 days later, those same disciples along with over 100 others were filled with the Holy Ghost on the Day of Pentecost to receive power *(Acts 1:8; 2:4)*, not salvation.

3. The Samaritan believers had already believed and been baptized in water *(Acts 8:12)*. According to how we believed, they had the Holy Ghost the moment they believed. Yet, days later Peter and John came to pray for them to receive the Holy Ghost, not salvation *(verse 14-17)*.

4. Paul asked the Ephesian believers in *Acts 19:1-2*, had they received the Holy Ghost since they believed. It's evident that they were saved because Paul acknowledged that they had believed. He asked had they received the Holy Ghost (notice, the Holy Ghost has to be received). That told me that this was another experience beyond salvation. When I am saved, I do not

have to receive the Holy Ghost, He comes to dwell in me automatically. This had to be another experience with the Holy Ghost.

5. *John 4:14* spoke of a well of water springing up into everlasting life. This is salvation.

6. *John 7:38-39* talks about believing on the Lord and then receiving the Holy Ghost. This experience was described as a river.

My theology was now totally shot out of the water. I saw that man's traditions were not consistent with the Word. Many times, we as Christians miss the blessings the Lord has for us because of our prejudiced, traditional mindsets. We believe what men have told us about God without ever consulting the Word of God. If everyone were honest, we would all have to admit that everything we know about God came from parents or preachers. Therefore, whatever understanding they had is what we have, whether right or wrong. I had to realize I never knew the God of the Bible for myself.

I found out that the initial biblical evidence of being filled with the Holy Ghost, was speaking in other tongues (see *Acts 2:4; Acts 10:44-46; Acts 19:1-6*). Although it does not mention tongues in the account with the Samaritans, we do know that Simon saw and heard something that made him want to buy this power *(Acts 8:17-19)*. So we know something had to have happened.

I saw that this experience with the Holy Ghost was for everyone that was saved, future generations and for anyone, no matter where they lived geographically.

I saw that the prophets validated the future of tongues *(Isaiah 28:11-12)*. Jesus and the Gospels sanctioned tongues *(Mark 16:17)*. Our denomination taught that when Jesus mentioned, "they shall speak with new tongues," He was talking about the results of being saved and how it will change one's talk. The word "tongues" in that passage is the Greek word *"glossalalia,"* which means a language not acquired by natural means. It cannot be learned, but is supernatural.

The historical New Testament book of *Acts* chronicles the beginning of the church and shows that tongues were a part of its inception. If this experience was a part of the early church, if this was the beginning of the church, the church today should be looking for the same thing. We are a part of that same church. If God has stopped tongues, He would have told us somewhere in scripture just as He told us that circumcision, the law, and animal sacrifices were no more.

The Apostle Paul testifies of his experience of speaking in tongues *(1 Corinthians 14:5,18)*. He stated his desire for everyone to speak in tongues and that probably no one spoke with tongues more than he.

The last great traditional hurdle or hindrance I had was that tongues were a gift for some and was not for everybody, and that there had to be an interpreter. Tongues for public worship is a gift only for some *(1 Corinthians 12:10)*. Everyone, however, has been given the gift of the Holy Ghost with the evidence of speaking in tongues for his or her own personal prayer life and devotional time with the Lord. Interpretation is only needed in church services for the body to understand *(1 Corinthians 14:5)*. During my personal prayer time, no interpretation is needed because I am not speaking to men, but unto God *(1 Corinthians 14:2)*. On the Day of Pentecost, it says they **ALL** spoke with tongues *(Acts 2:1-4)*, all 120 disciples *(Acts 1:15)*. If it was a gift for only a few, they should not have all spoken in tongues.

God lays claim on our tongues as a sign that He is now in control. The tongue gives expression to the things of our hearts. It is the one part of the body that man cannot tame *(James 3:8)*. When we are filled with the Spirit, He is saying to us "I am in control of your spirit (heart) now. I have control of the one thing you cannot control."

My doubts were now all gone. Even my questions about the different Baptisms were answered *(Please see Addendum A at the end of this chapter)*. My faith to receive came by hearing and hearing by the Word of God. Now I had to work on yielding my tongue.

I enrolled in Rhema, but I had yet to be filled. I was embarrassed that all of these students around me were filled with the Holy Ghost, but I wasn't. I tried praying for myself but nothing happened.

In the spring of the 1987-88 school year, I called a friend, Edward Slaughter, to come over to my house. He was someone who I felt I could trust to be open with about my failure in this area. He came over to our apartment one night to minister the Holy Ghost to my wife and me. He told us to ask the Holy Ghost to come upon us, to begin praising and thanking Him for this experience before anything took place. I remember thinking, "not this stuff again." My wife sat in a chair with her hands lifted up saying, "Thank you Jesus" over and over. In about two minutes, the Holy Ghost poured Himself out on her and she spoke immediately in a fluent tongue. While on the floor doing the same thing, I became so distracted with her experience until I could not concentrate on mine again. I went and hugged her because I was so happy for her. I later continued praising Him and uttered a few words. Slaughter would say to me, "That's right, that's right, you got it, keep on speaking." Once again I felt like an idiot. It sounded ridiculous to me. He told me that as I kept on speaking, the language would become more fluent and intelligible. Boy, I wasn't aware of all the hang-ups I had residing within me.

I was happy for my wife, yet, a little angry and jealous that she came through and I didn't, in the way I thought I should. I had to learn, however, that everyone's experience would not be with the same fluency. Most people do not get a full and fluent release at first. My wife had been exposed to this experience coming up in a Pentecostal background and did not have the hang-ups that I did. She always had a sensitivity to the things of the Spirit that I never had.

The mistake I made was, I was waiting for something to come take my tongue and move it for me. I wanted something to overtake me and make it happen. I learned I had to yield my tongue, open my mouth and begin speaking whatever sounds came out. The scriptures didn't say that the Holy Ghost spoke or the Holy Ghost made them speak. It says,

> "And THEY were all filled with the Holy Ghost and (THEY) BEGAN TO SPEAK WITH TONGUES.
>
> (Acts 2:4)

THE "TONGUES" ISSUE FINALLY SETTLED

My problem was that I did not ever accept by faith, that which I had received. I continued to compare my language with others. I finally went to Grace Fellowship Church in Tulsa, OK pastored by Pastor Bob Yandian. I asked to see him, but he was not there and I had to speak with an assistant. I told him what I had been through for almost three years. He prayed for me and once again it was a few words and nothing more. He told me, "Your problem is you have never believed that you have received. Accept that this is your prayer language. Walk in the awareness that God has filled you and begin to practice daily your prayer language." It was what I needed to hear and as the days went by, my language began to be more fluent and I began to sense more of God's presence as I used my language. The struggle was finally over. By faith I had received.

WHAT PRAYING IN TONGUES WILL DO FOR YOU

Praying in the Spirit *(1 Corinthians 14:14)* has brought me so much joy and made my joy full whenever I get spiritually weak. The power, wisdom and direction needed to pastor God's church has been phenomenal. What used to be a struggle for me has become sweatless victory. I had the ability to pray when I didn't know what to pray for *(Romans 8:26-27)* and knew the Holy Spirit was praying the will of God for me. God was giving me the utterance of what was to be prayed, which meant I was praying a perfect prayer that Satan could not understand. A new sense of boldness came when ministering God's Word or witnessing

22

for Him. I have a greater understanding of the scriptures. I see the things that God has freely given me by His Word that I could not see while looking through traditional eyes. My faith is built up to believe God. I have the ability to walk in authority over Satan and demons and cast them out. I witness the manifestation of the gifts of the Spirit. A deeper passion for souls and Jesus Christ has been glorified and revealed to me. You receive a desire and intensity to praise and worship the Lord like never before (see *Acts 4:31; 1 Corinthians 2:12; Jude 20; Luke 10:19-20; Mark 16:18; 1 Corinthians 12:1-11; Acts 2:14-41; Acts 1:8; John 14:21-23; 15:26; Hebrews 13:15; John 4:24*).

COMING HOME TO TEACH WHAT I LEARNED

      Finally, in February 1990, after returning back to Memphis from Tulsa, I began teaching the principles I had learned under the power of the Holy Ghost. Jesus told His disciples to tarry, and to not even try to operate in ministry until they had received the promise of the Father, the Baptism with the Holy Ghost *(Luke 24:49; Acts 1:4-5)* or power from on high.

  Jesus Himself did not began His ministry until He was anointed by the Holy Ghost *(Luke 3:22-23; Luke 4:1,14,18)*. The works and miracles He did were not because He was God, but because He was a man anointed and empowered by the Holy Ghost. That's why He tells us we can do the works that He did *(John 14:12)*. Jesus did not walk the earth those three and a half years as God, but as a man empowered by the Holy Ghost.

  When I came back, I saw people who had cancer with six months to live, 'be healed' and still living at the time of this writing. I saw tumors coughed up. I saw members who were told that they would have to have hysterectomies and while on the operating table, the tumors around the womb began to lift like cake.

  For about six or seven years after I returned ministering the Word of God on healing, no one under 70 years of age died in my church. Prior to going to Tulsa, we were having a funeral almost every week. I remember one week I had three.

MY DAUGHTER'S OPPRESSION

Finally, three months after returning to Memphis, we had a long overdue confrontation with the devil. I finally realized that my daughter's skin disease (atopic dermatitis) was not natural. There was a supernatural force present. It was hard to admit that my daughter was suffering from demonic oppression. I could not understand how an innocent child could have done anything to bring this upon herself. So the next thing I had to ask myself was what did I do that could have caused this problem for my child, as a parent *(John 9:2)*. I later found out that this spirit was sent as a messenger of Satan because of the Word and revelation I had received *(Mark 4:15; 2 Corinthians 12:7)*. It was sent to destroy or keep me distracted from my ministry. The Holy Ghost began to lead me through scriptures and other books to reveal that this was what we were dealing with. One night I got fed up with her waking up scratching in the middle of the night and not getting any sleep; I got tired of relying on doctors and medication to just get by for a while. The Holy Ghost rose up inside of me and I began to call those spirits out that night. The next night, little baby boils began to break out all over her body. We later found out that toxins were ridding themselves from her body. Once the spirits were gone, the body was free to react. Today, she is a healthy teenager. Since the night of confrontation, she has never bled again. We were in the doctor's office sometimes once a month or once every other month. We used to have to rub her down in cream 1 to 3 times a day, everyday. All of those things are now in the past. We saw a progressive healing and recovery take place *(Mark 16:17-18)*, all because of the power received by the Baptism with the Holy Ghost.

I thank God that I crossed tradition's line and got out of the boat.

ADDENDUM A

	THE BAPTISMAL EXPERIENCE	WHO WAS THE BAPTIZER	THE ELEMENT BAPTIZED IN	SCRIPTURE REFERENCES	PURPOSE
1	BAPTISM WITH WATER	MAN (Preacher)	WATER	*Acts 8:37-38* *John 1:31* *Matthew 3:13-16*	**IDENTIFICATION WITH CHRIST'S DEATH BURIAL & RESURRECTION** *Romans 6:3-4*
2	BAPTISM INTO THE BODY OF CHRIST	THE SPIRIT	THE BODY OF CHRIST (Salvation)	*1 Corinthians 12:13*	**SALVATION** *Ephesians 5:23* *Colossians 3:15*
3	BAPTISM WITH THE HOLY GHOST	JESUS	HOLY GHOST	*Matthew 3:11* *Mark 1:7-8* *Acts 1:4-5*	**POWER** *Acts 1:8* *Luke 24:49*

This is proof that baptism into the Body of Christ is a separate experience from the baptism with the Holy Ghost. If you go left to right, you will see that it is the Spirit that baptizes us into the Body of Christ (which is salvation), but it is Jesus (not the Spirit) that baptizes us with the Holy Ghost. One experience is for salvation and the other is for power.

3
DEFINING TRADITION

*"Then came to Jesus Scribes and Pharisees, which were of Jerusalem saying, 'Why do thy disciples transgress the **TRADITION** of the elders? For they wash not their hands when they eat bread."*
(Matthew 15:1-2)

The word *"elders"* literally means *"old men."* In this passage, the term refers to the ancient fathers or their ancestors. *"Tradition"* refers to something that has been handed down from one to another by memory; some precept or custom not commanded in the written law (Word), but which they held themselves bound to observe.

The Pharisees and all the Jews, except they "wash their hands oft, eat not." This custom of washing extended not merely to their hands before eating, but in coming from the market; and also to pots, cups, vessels and tables. They did this religiously for the sake of cleanliness. Ultimately it became a matter of superstition. **THEY REGARDED EXTERNAL PURITY AS OF MUCH MORE IMPORTANCE THAN THE PURITY OF THE HEART**. They had many foolish rules about it: how should the quantity be used; the way in which it should be applied; the number of times it should be changed; the number of those that might wash at one time, etc.

Jesus did not think it was proper for these foolish rules to be regarded or observed. This was the reason why they found fault with Him. They accused Jesus of violating their traditions as though they were obligatory. In His answer, He implied that they were not bound to obey their traditions because they were invented by men.

*"But he answered and said unto them, why do ye also transgress the commandment of God by your **TRADITION?***"

(Matthew 15:3)

Jesus said, those traditions could not be binding because they violated the commandments of God.

*"...Thus have ye made the commandment of God of none effect by your **TRADITION**."*

(Matthew 15:6)

*"**MAKING THE WORD OF GOD OF NONE EFFECT THROUGH YOUR TRADITION**, which ye have delivered: and many such like things to ye."*

(Mark 7:13)

In other words, the religious groups of Jesus' day imposed their traditions as equal in authority to the commands of God. They placed their denominational beliefs above God's Word. When men see the Bible through the eyes of their passed-down customs, it will not have any impact on people's lives. Here is something that, in this instance, is more powerful than the devil. The Word of God never says that the devil made the Word of God of none effect. Therefore, religion and tradition has power. It means you can read the scriptures and because of how your mind has been religiously brainwashed and indoctrinated, you cannot see the truth God desires for you to see.

Tradition would not let me see that Jesus is the same today as He was when He walked the earth *(Hebrews 13:8)*. Although I read the scriptures, my traditions blinded me from believing that God wanted me blessed, healed, prosperous, successful, joyful, peaceful, and walking in God's overcoming power. It was right there in the Word, but because my traditions said Jesus does not do that anymore and that the days of miracles are over, I bypassed those scriptures. I studied and preached only those subjects that were preached in my denomination. I saw the Word through my Baptist eyeglasses. I skipped over those things that were contrary to how my forefathers had taught me.

Tradition told me Jesus had changed. He no longer would heal the sick, cast out demons or deliver mankind from the powers of darkness. Tradition limited me to salvation, the forgiveness of sin and Heaven in the future. Therefore, the only message I could preach was something dealing with salvation, trials & tribulation, and going to Heaven. What you preach is what will happen in your church *(Mark 16:20)*. If salvation is all you preach, that's all people will have the faith to believe. So we waited and got through life the best we could, struggling and straining. Why? Because tradition said yesterday He cared for mankind – body, soul, and spirit, but He is not the same Savior today. Oh, He'll still save your spirit, but He leaves your body and soul ravaged by demons, strongholds and disease.

It's amazing how I preached that the Lord will make a way, Jesus will work it out, give it over to Jesus, and Jesus will see you through. Yet, when I ministered individually to my people, I gave them no hope. I subtly ministered doubt and unbelief to them because my tradition gave me no reason to believe.

*"And **HE COULD THERE DO NO MIGHTY WORK**, save that he laid his hands upon a few sick folk and healed them. And he marveled because of their **UNBELIEF**..."*

(Mark 6:5-6)

Jesus, the Son of God **COULD NOT** do any mighty work. Why? Unbelief. **TRADITION CAN STOP JESUS FROM DOING A MIGHTY WORK TODAY BECAUSE IT TRAINS YOU NOT TO BELIEVE ON HIM.** What was Jesus' remedy?

"...he went round about the villages, **TEACHING.**"

(Mark 6:6)

"Then came his disciples, and said unto him knowest thou that the Pharisees were offended, after they heard this saying? But he answered and said, 'EVERY PLANT, WHICH MY HEAVENLY FATHER HATH NOT PLANTED, SHALL BE ROOTED UP.'"
(Matthew 15:12-13)

Religious doctrines and tradition are being compared to a plant. It is planted in the mind for the purpose of producing fruit in the life or conduct. Jesus here says that all those doctrines of which his Father was not the author must be rooted up or corrected. The false doctrine of the Pharisees or religionists; therefore, had to be attacked. It was no wonder they were indignant. It could not be helped. They had to protect their following, their lies, and their money. He was not surprised by their outrage. But not withstanding their opposition, their doctrines should be destroyed. It was His duty to attack them.

"Let them alone: they be blind leaders of the blind. And if the blind lead the blind, both shall fall into the ditch."
(Matthew 15:14)

Religious, traditional leaders also lead the blind. They have great influence over the vast multitudes and they will usually become enraged at any doctrines that seek to lessen their authority or influence. Yet, multitudes of people are being led to ditches that lead to destruction. The Word of God says "...my people are destroyed for a lack of knowledge." (Hosea 4:6) This was the prime reason why Jesus confronted their errors and rooted up the religious plants of tradition, which God did not plant. By doing this, it would save and deliver the deluded multitudes. Jesus was tough on the religionists of His day. He called them full of dead men's bones, hypocrites, etc. (Matthew 23:27). Religious leaders came into a system only to duplicate what had already been done. They copied what had been taught and the style of those who have gone on before them. Most of these new leaders never had a genuine experience with the Lord for themselves. They never sought the Lord to find out what God had prepared for them to do, as well as, what He is doing today. Therefore, they rest on the laurels of the leadership of the past. Now the church becomes stuck in the things of the past.

THE DANGERS OF TRADITION

The reason religion and tradition are so dangerous is because of their ability to pacify their followers. The purpose of a baby's pacifier is to make him think he has the real thing by satisfying him with something that is an imitation of the real. That is exactly what religion does. It pacifies people and makes them think they have the real thing. As long as I go to church on Sunday and do a few outward religious duties, God must be satisfied with me. If I sing in the choir, teach Sunday school, or give a little money, surely God is pleased.

> *"Having a **FORM OF GODLINESS**,*
> ***BUT DENYING THE POWER*** *thereof:*
> *from such turn away."*
> *****(2 Timothy 3:5)*****

In other words, we profess religion and try to keep a connection with the church. We maintain a form of godliness, that is, we keep up with the forms of religion, but we deny the power behind our religion to make changes within. We end up becoming great church people, but we are wretched, miserable, poor, blind and naked within *(Revelation 3:17)*.

> *"This people draweth nigh unto me with their mouth and honoureth me with their lips;**BUT THEIR HEART IS FAR FROM ME."***
> *****(Matthew 15:8)*****

They say all the right things, they speak all of the religious jargon, and they give grand testimonies to try to prove that God is with them. They are regular in the forms of worship. They are strict in ceremonial observances and keep the law outwardly, but God requires the heart, and that, they have not rendered. That's why many can't handle teaching on sin, repentance, the Holy Ghost, tongues, praise, worship and lifting of hands. These things will make you deal with the heart.

*"But **IN VAIN THEY DO WORSHIP ME**, teaching for doctrines, the commandments of men."*
(Matthew 15:9)

That is, their attempts to worship are vain or are not real worship - they are mere forms. They teach for doctrines, the requirements of their religion, denomination or traditions, the things they want their people to believe and practice. Only God has the right to declare what shall be done in His service, but they held their traditions to be superior to the written Word of God and taught their doctrines to bind their conscience. I would hate to find out that my weekly worship of God was in vain and not accepted by Him.

TRADITION'S WALLS ARE CRUMBLING

Tradition will blind men to their basic spiritual need by making the observance of many external forms as the essential qualifications to be accepted with God. This book has been written with the intent of pulling you out of the dark hole of tradition, so that you will no longer be chained and shackled by the teachings of men. I thank God that He set me free from the spirit behind the traditions of men. Many denominational people and pastors are experiencing this same freedom. The walls of tradition are crumbling before the Word of God. Those walls are not high enough or strong enough to hold the desperate yet hungry people in this dark hour of human history. People are hearing the sound of a distant drummer calling for them to come out of religion and tradition and march to the tune of the Word of God. People are sensing that there is something more than what their religion has been giving them.

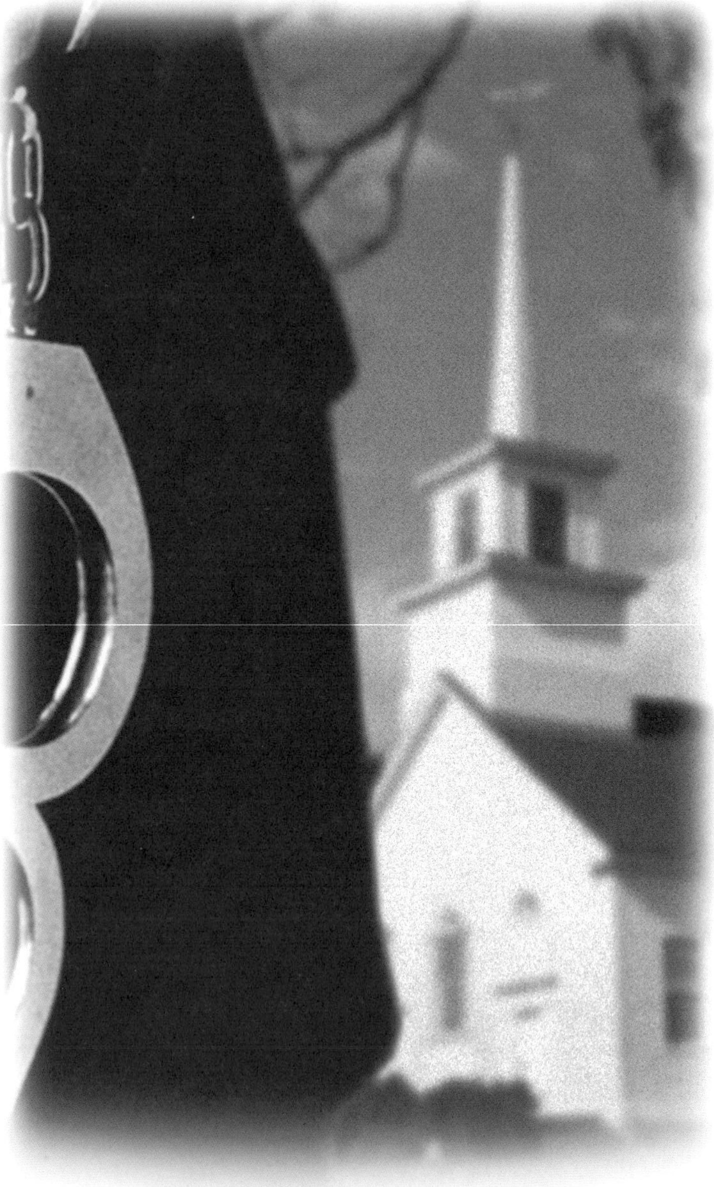

4

TRADITIONS OF THE CHURCH

The following is an example of some of the many traditions, doctrines, teachings and mindsets of men that have been passed down through generations. Most of these are totally inconsistent with the Word of God. (*Note*: This is not an exhaustive list. There are many church traditions. The following are some of the most familiar.

✦ 1. **I'M JUST A SINNER SAVED BY GRACE** *(Romans 1:7; Romans 6:1-14; 1 Peter 4:1-3; 1 John 3:6-10; 1 John 5:18). This statement implies that a person is still a sinner.*

✦ 2. **GOD WANTS ME TO BE HAPPY; I ONLY HAVE ONE LIFE TO LIVE** *(Psalm 128:1-4; Proverbs 28:14; Proverbs 29:18b; James 5:10-11; 1 Peter 3:14).*

✦ 3. **GOD WILL NOT JUDGE ME. ISN'T GOD A GOD OF LOVE?** *(John 14:21,23; 1 John 4:7-9; 1 John 5:3; 1 Corinthians 11:31-32).*

✦ 4. **GOD UNDERSTANDS AND KNOWS THAT I'M GOING TO SIN; HIS GRACE HAS GOT ME COVERED** *(Romans 6:1-14; 1 Peter 4:1-2; 1 John 3:6-10; Jude 4).*

✦ 5. YOU CAN NEVER EVER, UNDER ANY CIRCUM-STANCE LOSE YOUR SALVATION, NO MATTER WHAT YOU DO *(Colossians 1:22-23; Hebrews 3:12-14; 1 Timothy 4:16; 1 Peter 1:4-5; James 5:19-20; 1 John 2:23; 2 John 9).*

✦ 6. WHEN I GOT SAVED, THE HOLY GHOST CAME TO DWELL IN ME AND THAT'S THE ONLY EXPERIENCE WITH THE HOLY GHOST I WILL EVER NEED *(Acts 1:4-5,9; Acts 2:4; Acts 19:1-2; Acts 8:12-17).*

✦ 7. WE GOT TO KEEP ON WORKING FOR THE LORD SO WE CAN GET INTO HEAVEN *(Romans 3:20-27; Romans 4:6; Galatians 2:16; Ephesians 2:8-9; Titus 3:5).*

✦ 8. AS LONG AS YOU ARE SAVED AND GOING TO HEAVEN, YOU CAN DO WHATEVER YOU WANT TO DO. YOU ARE NOT GOING TO DIE UNTIL YOUR TIME COMES ANYWAY *(Ecclesiastes 7:17; Ezekiel 18:23-32; Deuteronomy 30:19; Romans 6:23; Proverbs 9:10-11).*

✦ 9. IF YOU DIDN'T FEEL SOMETHING WHEN YOU CAME TO RECEIVE JESUS, SOMETHING IS WRONG WITH YOU *(Ephesians 2-9; Romans 10:9,13; John 3:16; Matthew 9:29; 1 John 5:13).*

✦ 10. IF YOU COMMITTED SIN ON SATURDAY NIGHT, MAKE SURE YOU GO TO CHURCH AND DO SOMETHING DOUBLE FOR THE LORD SO HE WILL FORGIVE YOU *(Ephesians 2:8-9; 1 John 1:9; Titus 3:5).*

✦ 11. LET'S GET BACK TO OUR ROOTS AND SING ALL OF OUR OLD SONGS AND HYMNS LIKE WE USE TO *(Isaiah 42:9-10; Isaiah 43:18-19; Mark 7:13; Psalm 98:1).*

✦ 12. **LET'S PRAY THAT GOD MAKES OUR CHURCH WHAT IT USE TO BE UNDER OUR FORMER PASTOR** *(Philippians 3:13-14; Isaiah 43:18-19).*

✦ 13. **THE LORD WON'T PUT NO MORE ON HIS CHILDREN THAN THEY CAN BEAR.** *(1 Corinthians 10:13; John 10:10; 1 Thessalonians 3:3-5; 1 Peter 5:7-8)*

✦ 14. **YOU MUST BE BAPTIZED BY A BAPTIST, METHODIST OR PRESBYTERIAN MINISTER TO BE SAVED.** *(Mark 16:16; Acts 8:12-16; Acts 18:7-8)*

✦ 15. **WE MUST VOTE ON PEOPLE TO BE A MEMBER BEFORE THEY CAN BE A PART OF THIS CHURCH.** *(Romans 12:4-5; 1 Corinthians 12:12-14; Ephesians 3:14-15; Hebrews 3:6)*

✦ 16. **GOD PUT THESE TRIALS ON ME SO HE COULD MAKE ME STRONGER.** *(Proverbs 24:5,10; James 1:2-4,13; 1 Thessalonians 3:3-5)*

✦ 17. **THE LORD GIVETH AND THE LORD TAKETH AWAY** *(Job 1:12-19; Luke 9:56; John 10:10; Hebrews 2:14; 1 Peter 5:8).*

✦ 18. **GOD TOOK MY HUSBAND IN ORDER TO MAKE ME GET CLOSER TO HIM** *(John 10:10; Job 1:12-19; James 4:8; John 8:44; Hebrews 2:14).*

✦ 19. **GOD MADE ME SICK IN ORDER TO PUNISH ME** *(Luke 10:9; Acts 10:38; Luke 13:16; James 1:13; Deuteronomy 7:15).*

✦ 20. **MIRACLES WENT AWAY WITH THE APOSTLES** *(1 Corinthians 12:10,28; Hebrews 13:8).*

✦ 21. **HEALING ISN'T FOR EVERYBODY; ONLY SOME GET LUCKY** *(Isaiah 53:5; Matthew 12:15; James 5:14-15; 1 Peter 2:24).*

✦ 22. **LORD, JUST TAKE SOME OF MY BURDENS AND CARES AWAY** *(1 Peter 5:7; Psalm 55:22; Matthew 11:30).*

✦ 23. **GOD HEALS IF IT IS HIS WILL.** *(1 John 5:14; Luke 5:12-13; John 6:38; Acts 10:38).*

✦ 24. **I'VE JUST LEARNED TO GIVE GOD GLORY IN MY SICKNESS** *(Matthew 15:31; Luke 5:24-26; Luke 13:13).*

✦ 25. **GOD WAS THE ONE WHO KILLED MY MOTHER** *(Ecclesiastes 7:17; Ezekiel 18:21-32; John 10:10; 1 Peter 5:8; Hebrews 2:14).*

✦ 26. **GOD IS THE CAUSE OF ALL ACCIDENTS, TRAGEDIES AND DISASTERS THAT HAPPEN TO PEOPLE** *(1 Kings 10:11-12; Job 1:12-19; Proverbs 1:20-33; Luke 9:54-56; John 10:10; 1 Peter 5:8; Mark 4:37-41).*

✦ 27. **EVERYTHING GOOD OR BAD THAT HAPPENED TO ME, GOD DID IT, MEANT IT TO BE AND ALREADY PREDESTINED IT TO HAPPEN BEFORE I WAS BORN** *(Deuteronomy 28:15; Deuteronomy 30:19; Luke 13:16; James 1:17).*

✦ 28. **MY PROBLEMS AND SICKNESSES WERE JUST THE CARDS GOD DEALT ME IN LIFE. I MIGHT AS WELL ACCEPT IT. IT'S JUST THE CROSS I'VE GOT TO BEAR** *(Joshua 1:8; Deuteronomy 30:19; Psalm 55:22; Isaiah 43:2; Luke 13:16; John 16:33; Acts 10:38; 1 John 3:8; 1 John 5:4-5; James 4:7; John 8:37; 2 Corinthians 2:14).*

✦ 29. **GOD CHOOSES SOME PEOPLE TO SUCCEED AND OTHERS TO FAIL** *(Joshua 1:8; Deuteronomy 30:19; Deuteronomy 28:15,20; Psalm 1:1-3).*

✦ 30. **GOD USES SICKNESS TO CHASTISE AND TEACH ME SOME THINGS** *(Psalm 103:1-4; Psalm 94:12; Acts 10:38; James 5:14-15).*

✦ 31. **THIS SICKNESS IS MY THORN IN THE FLESH** *(Paul's thorn was the messenger of Satan and in other places in the Bible it refers to groups of people and never sickness – 2 Corinthians 12:7; Numbers 33:55; Joshua 23:13).*

✦ 32. **YOU ONLY NEED A LITTLE FAITH, THE SIZE OF A MUSTARD SEED** *(The scripture never said "size," but AS a mustard seed. God does not delight in little faith, but great faith). (Matthew 17:20; Matthew 8:26; Matthew 15:28).*

✦ 33. **IN ORDER TO GET SAVED, YOU GIVE GOD YOUR HEART AND THE PREACHER YOUR HAND** *(Romans 10:9,13; Hebrews 10:10-16; 1 Peter 2:9).*

✦ 34. **IT'S EITHER HOLINESS OR HELL. HOLINESS IS REQUIRED FOR SALVATION** *(John 3:16,18,36; Romans 3:20-27; Romans 10:9,13; Hebrews 10:14; Romans 5:9-10).*

✦ 35. **I'M ABOVE EVER SINNING AGAIN BECAUSE I'M SAVED, SANCTIFIED AND FILLED WITH THE HOLY GHOST** *(Romans 7:14-25; John 17:17; 1 John 1:8; Leviticus 20:7-8; Romans 5:9-10; 1 Thessalonians 5:23).*

✦ 36. **IF YOU SIN, YOU MUST GET SAVED ALL OVER AGAIN** *(1 John 1:9; Hebrews 10:10,14; 1 John 2:1-2; Romans 5:9-10; Colossians 2:13; John 5:24).*

✦ 37. **IF YOU ARE GOING TO GET SAVED, YOU HAVE GOT TO GIVE UP SOME THINGS** *(Ephesians 2:8-9; Titus 3:5; Romans 5:17-18).*

✦ 38. WOMEN CAN'T PREACH IN THE CHURCH, NEITHER SHOULD THEY TEACH OR BE IN LEADERSHIP OVER A MAN *(Luke 2:36-38; 1 Corinthians 11:5; 1 Corinthians 14:4; Judges 4:4, 6-9, Romans 16:1-3).*

✦ 39. YOU MUST TARRY FOR THE HOLY GHOST *(Acts 8:14-17; Acts 10:44-46; Acts 19:1-6).*

✦ 40. WOMEN CANNOT WEAR THAT WHICH PERTAINETH TO A MAN (PANTS) *(Deuteronomy 22:5)* – *This scripture has references to what we know today as cross dressers, homosexuals and transvestites.*

✦ 41. GOD IS AGAINST WOMEN WEARING MAKEUP BECAUSE THAT'S WHAT JEZEBEL DID. *(Jezebel was not judged for makeup. God judged her for her idolatry, hatred of His prophets, witchcraft and her whoredoms (2 Kings 9:22; 1 Kings 16:31; 1 Kings 18:4). Job's third daughter that God gave him after he was delivered was named Kerenhappuch, which means "horn of cosmetic", "to paint ones eyes" (Job 42:14). (See also 1 Samuel 16:7; Revelation 2:20-21).*

✦ 42. YOU CANNOT BE SAVED UNLESS YOU SPEAK IN TONGUES *(Romans 10:9,13; Romans 3:20-27; Mark 16:16; Acts 19:1-6). Tongues should follow after you have believed (Mark 16:17).*

✦ 43. WOMEN MUST WEAR A COVERING OVER THEIR HEADS *(1 Corinthians 11:13-16).*

✦ 44. YOU CAN'T SPEAK IN TONGUES UNLESS SOMETHING COMES OVER YOU AND MAKES YOU SPEAK *(1 Corinthians 14:14-15).*

✦ 45. IF YOU LEAVE OUR CHURCH, SOMETHING BAD IS GOING TO HAPPEN TO YOU *(Psalm 34:7; Proverbs 1:33; Proverbs 29:25; Psalm 118:6; Luke 9:56)*.

✦ 46. WOMEN SHOULD NOT ADORN THEMSELVES OR TRY TO LOOK BEAUTIFUL. LOOKING BEAUTIFUL WILL CAUSE MEN TO LUST *(1 Peter 3:3-4; Ezekiel 16:8-14; Genesis 24:22,30; Esther 1:11)*.

✦ 47. SEX IS ONLY FOR HAVING CHILDREN AND IS NOT TO BE ENJOYED *(Genesis 18:12; Proverbs 5:19; Song of Solomon 4-5; 1 Corinthians 7:4-5)*.

✦ 48. RICH PEOPLE CAN'T GO TO HEAVEN *(Genesis 13:2; Luke 16:22-24; Genesis 14:23; 2 Corinthians 8:9; Proverbs 11:28; Psalm 112:3)*.

✦ 49. THERE SHOULD BE NO MUSICAL INSTRUMENTS IN THE CHURCH *(Acts 15:16-17; What was in the tabernacle of David? - Psalm 150:1-5; 2 Chronicles 29:26-28)*.

✦ 50. THE LORD MOVES IN MYSTERIOUS WAYS. NO ONE CAN KNOW THE MYSTERIES AND WAYS OF GOD. *(Luke 8:10; Ephesians 1:9; Mark 4:11; Matthew 13:11)*.

✦ 51. NO ONE CAN UNDERSTAND GOD'S WORD; IT'S TOO HARD *(Proverbs 4:5,7; Matthew 13:23)*.

✦ 52. YOU MUST BE BAPTIZED IN ORDER TO BE SAVED *(Luke 23:42-43; Acts 10:45; Romans 10:9,13)*.

✦ 53. YOU MUST BE BAPTIZED IN JESUS' NAME ONLY *(Matthew 28:19)*.

✦ 54. JESUS IS THE FATHER AND THE HOLY GHOST. THERE IS NO TRINITY. WE BELIEVE IN THE UNITY OF THE SON. THEY ARE ALL THE SAME. *(When Jesus was on earth, the Holy Ghost was coming down and the Father was in Heaven) (Matthew 3:16-17). Jesus came not to do his own will, but the Father's will (John 6:37-38). Jesus had to send the Holy Ghost (John 16:7; Matthew 26:39).*

✦ 55. DIVORCE IS THE UNPARDONABLE SIN AND CANNOT BE FORGIVEN *(Deuteronomy 24:1-4; Matthew 19:7-8,10-11; 1 John 1:9; 1 Corinthians 7:27-28).*

✦ 56. IF YOU DIVORCE AND REMARRY, YOU WILL BE COMMITTING ADULTERY AND FOREVER LIVING IN SIN *(Deuteronomy 24:1-4; 1 Corinthians 7:27-28; 1 John 1:9).*

✦ 57. IF YOU DON'T GO TO CHURCH ON SATURDAY, THE SABBATH OR SEVENTH DAY, YOU ARE NOT SAVED *(Colossians 2:16-17; Matthew 12:3-8; Romans 14:5-6; 1 Corinthians 16:1-2; Mark 16:1-2,9)*

✦ 58. GOD IS A HARD AND ANGRY GOD WHO PUNISHES AND BEATS UP ON US *(Psalm 86:5,7; Micah 7:18-19; Psalm 136:1-26).*

✦ 59. SPEAKING IN TONGUES IS OF THE DEVIL *(Acts 2:4; Luke 11:11-13; Luke 10:19; Serpents and scorpions are symbolic of devils and demons).*

✦ 60. WE ONLY BAPTIZE BY SPRINKLING *(Acts 8:38; Romans 6:3).*

✦ 61. WE BELIEVE IN INFANT BAPTISM *(Mark 16:16 – only those who believe should be baptized).*

✦ 62. YOU MUST CONFESS YOUR SINS TO A PRIEST TO BE FORGIVEN *(1 John 1:9; Hebrews 9:6,12, 15; Hebrews 4:16; Hebrews 10:16-22; Hebrews 7:22-28).*

✦ 63. ONLY THE POPE CAN FORGIVE SIN *(Hebrews 9:11-28; Hebrews 10:17-19; 1 John 1:9; Colossians 2:13-14; Luke 5:21,24).*

✦ 64. WE MUST GO TO PURGATORY AND BE PUNISHED A WHILE BEFORE GOING TO HEAVEN *(2 Corinthians 5:8; Philippians 1:21-24; 1 Thessalonians 4:13-18; 1 Corinthians 15:51-55; Psalm 116:15; Revelation 14:13).*

✦ 65. A PRIEST SHOULD NOT MARRY *(1 Timothy 4:1-3; 1 Corinthians 7:7-9).*

✦ 66. WHEN WE DIE, WE CEASE TO EXIST *(Philippians 1:21; 2 Corinthians 5:8; Luke 16:19-31).*

✦ 67. DEVILS, DEMONS AND EVIL SPIRITS ARE NOT REAL *(Jesus said they are —Mark 16:17; Matthew 10:8; Luke 11:13,16).*

✦ 68. THERE ARE NO REAL ANGELS *(Jesus says there are—Matthew 18:10; Luke 16:22; Mark 13:32; Hebrews 1:13-14; Hebrews 13:2; Psalm 91:11; Psalm 34:7).*

✦ 69. WHEN WE GO TO HEAVEN, WE BECOME LIKE ANGELS *(1 Corinthians 6:3; Revelation 3:21; Revelation 7:11).*

✦ 70. WHEN WE GO TO HEAVEN, WE WILL JUST BE FLOATING AROUND IN SPACE *(Revelation 7:15; Revelation 2:7,17,26; 3:21).*

✦ 71. THE DEVIL CAN'T HURT ME; HE HAS NO POWER *(Acts 26:18; Colossians 1:13; Luke 22:53; 1 Peter 5:8; Luke 9:42; Mark 1:32-34; John 10:10).*

✦ 72. IF YOU DON'T BOTHER THE DEVIL, HE WON'T BOTHER YOU *(Mark 4:15; Ephesians 6:12-13,16; 1 John 5:18).*

✦ 73. EATING PORK IS A SIN *(1 Timothy 4:1-5; 1 Corinthians 6:12; Romans 14:3; 1 Corinthians 8:8; Mark 7:15,18-20).*

✦ 74. SPEAKING IN TONGUES IS NOT FOR TODAY. IT CEASED WITH THE DEATH OF THE APOSTLES *(1 Corinthians 13:8-12; 1 Corinthians 12:10).*

✦ 75. GOD WANTS US TO BE POOR BECAUSE MONEY WILL KEEP YOU FROM BEING HUMBLE *(Proverbs 10:22; Proverbs 11:28; Proverbs 10:4; 2 Corinthians 8:9).*

✦ 76. JESUS WAS POOR. HE HAD NO HOME BECAUSE HE HAD NOWHERE TO LAY HIS HEAD *(Luke 9:58; John 1:37-39).*

✦ 77. WHENEVER SOMEONE SPEAKS IN TONGUES, THERE MUST BE AN INTERPRETER *(1 Corinthians 14:2,5 – an interpreter is only needed in church, not when I am personally or privately talking to God).*

✦ 78. IF THE PREACHER DOESN'T HOOP, HOLLER, AND TUNE, YOU WON'T HAVE A CHURCH *(1 Timothy 3:2; Matthew 28:19; Mark 6:6; Mark 12:35,37).*

✦ 79. CHILDREN SHOULD NOT ACCEPT OR COME TO THE LORD *(Matthew 19:14).*

✦ 80. **THE WINE AND BREAD OF THE LORD'S SUPPER WHEN RECEIVED ACTUALLY BECOMES THE REAL BODY AND BLOOD OF THE LORD** *(Acts 7:55; 1 Corinthians 11:23-26; Mark 14:22-24 – We could not be eating Jesus up because He is still in Heaven. Even when Jesus was here, He did not drink His own blood and eat His own body. He hasn't come back yet).*

✦ 81. **TITHING IS UNDER THE LAW OF MOSES AND IS NOT FOR THE NEW TESTAMENT CHURCH** *(Tithing is a universal, eternal principle established before the law and for the New Testament believer. Genesis 14:19-20; Matthew 23:23; Hebrews 7:5-9).*

✦ 82. **IF YOU CANNOT TITHE, JUST GIVE AN OFFERING OR WHATEVER YOU CAN. GOD UNDERSTANDS AND KNOWS YOUR HEART** *(Deuteronomy 14:28; Malachi 3:8-11; Malachi 1:6-10; Luke 12:34).*

✦ 83. **YOU MUST KEEP THE LAW IN ORDER TO BE SAVED** *(Galatians 2:16; Romans 3:20).*

✦ 84. **"GOD, I COME TO YOU AS HUMBLE AS I KNOW HOW, KNEE BENT AND BODY BOWED. I KNOW I'M NOT DESERVING AND I'M NOT WORTHY TO COME TO YOU."** *(Hebrews 4:16; Hebrews 10:17-19).*

✦ 85. **IT TAKES YEARS TO BECOME SPIRITUALLY MATURE IN ORDER TO BE RIGHTEOUS. YOU MUST WORK YOUR WAY TO PERFECTION IN ORDER TO BE RIGHTEOUS BEFORE GOD** *(Romans 3:22; Romans 4:5; Romans 5:15-19; James 5:16-18).*

✦ 86. **GOD ANSWERS PRAYER IN THREE WAYS: YES, NO OR MAYBE** *(1 John 5:14; 2 Corinthian 1:20; Psalm 66:18; Matthew 7:7-8; Mark 11:23-24; John 16:23).*

THE DAY I USED ANOTHER MAN'S TRADITIONS

There have been times in my ministry when God showed me that my doctrinal, denominational sacred cows did not matter to Him. As a young Baptist preacher, like those before me, I taught that we do not sprinkle when baptizing, as do the Methodist and other denominations. Of course, we taught baptism by immersion, which is what I believe the scriptures teach. God showed me, however, that the Spirit gives life, and abiding by the letter of the law killeth.

I remember one Sunday; a woman came to receive the Lord at our church. She wanted to be baptized but could not go under water because she had a tracheotomy in her throat. Going under water of course would allow water to get in. I was now faced with a situation where I could not keep my denomination's form or mode of baptism by immersion. I had to use sprinkling, something I denounced many times. God honored that woman's faith that day and life was ministered to her. She needed the assurance of knowing that she had obeyed what God asked her to do. I learned that day, that we cannot get too hung up in our traditions. After all, it's the repentance and belief that gets you saved. Just ask the thief on the cross *(Mark 1:15; Romans 10:9,13, Luke 23:42-43)*.

FINDING WHAT GOD HAS PREPARED FOR YOU

Praise God, there has arisen a generation of believers that will dare to believe God. You are a part of that generation and shall have your share of God's power to enable you to fulfill His perfect will in your life. However, tradition will block you from finding your divine purpose and assignment. Why? Because tradition will not teach you the ways of God, His mind and His purposes. Tradition will only teach you the ways of men or the denomination.

> *"But as it is written, Eye hath not seen, nor ears heard, neither have entered into the heart of man,* **THE THINGS WHICH GOD HATH PREPARED FOR THEM THAT LOVE HIM."**
>
> ***(1 Corinthians 2:9)***

This is not a funeral scripture, as it is used in many church circles. God has prepared some great things for those who love Him in this life. How do we find the things that have been prepared for us?

> *"...God hath* **REVEALED THEM** *unto us* **BY HIS SPIRIT:"**
>
> ***(1 Corinthians 2:10a)***

*"Now we have received, not the spirit of the world, but the Spirit which is of God; **THAT WE MIGHT KNOW THE THINGS THAT ARE FREELY GIVEN TO US OF GOD.**"*

(1 Corinthians 2:12)

*"Which things also we speak, not in the words which **MAN'S WISDOM TEACHETH**, but which the **HOLY HOST TEACHETH**; comparing spiritual things with spiritual"*

(verse 13)

This proves that this passage is not speaking of those believers who have died. Why? Because there will be no teaching of man's wisdom in Heaven. If a church, however, is not taught the ways of the Holy Ghost, it will never see the things that God has freely given to them, such as: healing, deliverance, prosperity, blessings, assignments, answered prayer, faith, the love of God, miracles, and power.

We do not need to be proselytized into another denomination. We don't want to be fitted into another doctrinal mold that someone may gloat over them as converts. It's time to climb the hill of God and get above the fog and smog of tradition and religion. We must have the power of His Spirit. We want more than religion. We want the miracle life of God that comes through the mighty Baptism in the Holy Ghost. We've got to have God's miracle working power that will enable us to effectively reach the lost, doomed, and dying before it is everlastingly too late!

ARE YOU AT A SPIRITUAL CROSSROAD?

Have you come to the point in your church life where you feel that there is something more? Do you feel as though you are not being fed? Are you in a church that you do not want to be in, but because of your family loyalties you just can't seem to leave? Have you said, "I can't leave the church where I was baptized, married or where my parents went, were married or funeralized"; yet, you are not sensing more of God in your life? Have you been to a church where you experienced the presence of God or tasted the good Word of God, and now your old church doesn't feel the same? Are you at a church where you are not spiritually fulfilled, yet you can't let go because of a position that you hold in that church? Instead of leaving, you've taken the position that you will stay and pray for the pastor to change. Going to another church may mean that it will take you years to get back to the top. Are you fed up with a lot of church works? If so, you are at a crossroad in your spiritual life.

Pastors, do you want more than what you have? Are you tired of being influenced and/or controlled by other preachers? Are you tired of the religious competitive games among your peers? You know that there is something more to pastoring, but are you afraid to step out? Are you scared to preach things outside of your denominational doctrine? Are you dry within? Do you desire to see more life and intensity in your service? Do you desire to help your people more? Do you get hungry for more intimate fellowship with Jesus? Then my dear pastor, you are a candidate for change.

I have been through most of these things and more in my efforts to come out of tradition. I will admit to you, it is not easy to overcome religion and tradition, however, it is definitely not impossible. It is my desire to assist you in making some crucial decisions for your life, the life of your children and future generations to come *(Deuteronomy 30:19)*. You are at a "fork in the road," in your spiritual life or at an intersection, trying to decide which way to go. You realize that it is time for a change, but you are allowing reasons, excuses, or people to hold you in a spiritual prison. **IT'S TIME TO COME OUT.** Your choices today are forming your future.

CHOICES DETERMINE THE QUALITY OF LIFE

"I call heaven and earth to record this day against you, that I have set before you life and death, blessing and cursing: therefore ***CHOOSE LIFE, THAT BOTH THOU AND THY SEED MAY LIVE:***

(Deuteronomy 30:19)

God has established in His Word everything we must do in order to have life or that which will bring blessing into our lives. He tells us what to choose but leaves it up to us as to what we will choose. God will not choose for us, neither will He force us to make those choices.

When you see people who are blessed in life, it is because they have made some good choices that produced life or good results. On the other hand, when you see cursing, evil, lack, sorrow, and unhappiness as a pattern in a person's life, it's due to bad choices made by that person or sometimes, even ancestors before them. *(Exodus 20:5)*

Everything begins with our choices. Even when you do not choose to do anything, you are still making a choice. Therefore, when a person has chosen to follow God and His Word at all costs, he or she has made the ultimate choice that will dictate life's personal day-to-day decisions. Once God becomes priority in a person's life, he will desire to choose those things that will please God.

Whatever your life is today, it is a result of the choices you made: You chose that spouse that has now given you so much hell. You chose not to go to school to better your job skills. Yes, your parents did or said things that hurt you or set your life behind, but somewhere along the way, you chose to let it bother you or not forgive and be bitter. You chose the church you are in and chose to stay in it even after your parents died. Even when you don't choose, you are making a choice. To stay in tradition, especially when God has presented you with another choice that will give you life, is to choose death or cursing. **TRADITION CAN'T GIVE ME LIFE, ONLY GOD'S WORD CAN.**

CHOOSING THE KNOWLEDGE OF GOD

"My people are destroyed for lack of knowledge:
BECAUSE THOU HAST REJECTED KNOWLEDGE,
I WILL ALSO REJECT THEE*, that thou shalt be*
no priest to me: seeing thou has forgotten the
law of thy God, I will also forget thy children."

(Hosea 4:6)

When knowledge of God's Word is not a priority in our lives; when there is not a desire to know His will, promises, plans and purposes, God has no reason to respond to us because we have shown Him by our actions that we are not interested in Him *(Proverbs 1:20-33)*. Seeking the knowledge of God is another choice. The only way we get to know God is through knowledge of Him through His Word. I will speak more on this later.

That's why choosing the right church that will feed you with knowledge and understanding is a vital decision. It is a vital choice. It does matter where you go to church. The scriptures speak of *"taking heed to what you hear."* If you are at a church and all you hear is doubt, unbelief, no belief in the supernatural, no expectation of God changing situations and circumstances in your life; you never receive any understanding of the Word of God; if you do not see yourself being conformed more to the image of Christ, then you are in the wrong church.

In 1987, I was faced with a choice that would ultimately determine my destiny. God challenged me to choose between my personal ambitions for my own life, for the life He had for me. I was faced with choosing between God's plan for my life and keeping my family happy. I had to choose between the church traditions of my family or the direction I sensed the Holy Spirit of God leading me. I had to choose between God's predestined plan for my life and the expectations that pastors and ministers of the city had of me, because of whose son and brother I was. I had been offered a position among the ministers just because of whose son I was.

HIS PREDESTINED PLAN ORDERED MY STEPS

*"In whom also **WE HAVE OBTAINED AN INHERITANCE, BEING PREDESTINATED** according to the purpose of him who worketh all things after the counsel of his own will:"*

(Ephesians 1:11)

"Order my steps in thy word: and let not any iniquity have dominion over me."

(Psalm 119:133)

God's inheritance for your life can only be found after you locate the predestinated plan for your life. God has predetermined your life's call, purpose, and assignment in Him. Once you realize that things are not going right or working according to your own plans and you begin to seek God for answers, He slowly begins to order your steps. After each step of obedience, He gives you another step until He is finally able to place you in the place he has always purposed for you to be in. Looking back I found that I was at my "fork in the road." I had become restless in my personal life and ministry. My route and the route family and man had planned for me were not working. I found out that there was another route. And oh, when I finally got on that road, I found what God had predestined my life to do. As a result, I found the inheritance that goes along with obeying His plan. It took prayer, understanding of His Word, faith, seeking Him, obeying Him, etc.

There is a predestinated plan already set for your life before you were ever born.

***"BEFORE I FORMED THEE IN THE BELLY,** I knew thee; and before thou camest forth out of the womb **I SANCTIFIED THEE, AND I ORDAINED THEE** a prophet unto the nations."*

(Jeremiah 1:5)

You can try to pastor just because that's what all the other guys do when they sense a call. You will not succeed, however, if God has not called you to do it. Many ministers were never called to pastor. It was just the thing to do. If you've been called to preach, you go out get a church so you can have somewhere to exercise your gift and preach every Sunday. Then when things are not working, we spend a lifetime praying to God to come in and make everything go right. If God never called you to pastor to begin with, it will not work because you are out of place. Sometimes God's permissive plan will allow you to be placed in these situations, yet, it is not His perfect will for your life.

When you are in the permissive will of God, ministry is a struggle. There is no peace; you are never fulfilled. In the perfect will of God, however, there is peace even in the midst of storms and trials. There is an inner knowing that whatever tough places you are in, God will bring you out, because you are where you are supposed to be.

I tried to preach like my father and brother. I never had inner peace no matter how many people shouted when I hooped and hollered. I did not find fulfillment in my ministry until I got in God's predestined plan for my life, and that was to stand in the office of teacher *(Ephesians 4:11-12)*. It was a difficult transition to make because most black Baptist congregations loved inspiration more than information. They loved preaching more than teaching on how to live. I also knew teaching the Word would begin to challenge their lifestyles, and people did not want to change their lives.

I remember the Sunday I finally stopped the performance. I am not saying that whenever a minister hoops, he is performing. It was performance for me because I was imitating someone else and was not doing what God called me to do. I was on the program to preach the message at the anniversary of a well-known pastor in Memphis. I preached my message; everyone waited for the close. People would holler, "yeah," just to hurry you on to the tuning part. This Sunday, I said what I had to say and I just sat down. People were shocked. The place was quiet. "You mean he didn't hoop, He's a *'Williams'*". It was expected of me to do as those who had gone before me, but I was tired of saying what I heard others say. I was tired of playing on people's emotions just so I could leave out feeling I had done something. I got tired of being who I wasn't. I got tired of trying to act like my daddy and brother, just to please people. I got tired of saying what made them feel good at the moment, rather than change their lives.

When that service was over and I sat in the pastor's office with some other preachers, the TV was on and Dr. Fred Price was on teaching. I remember telling them, "That's what I have been called to do." That was my last time preaching at that church.

Oh, but when I began to get in the predestined plan that God had for my life, my ministry changed and I found my inheritance. When I began teaching and giving people understanding, regardless of what their ears itched to hear, God multiplied His people unto me and enlarged my tent *(Isaiah 43:4-5; Isaiah 54:2)*.

When God begins to move in your life, you will be challenged to make Him and His will priority in your life. God will begin to speak to you, lead you and guide you once you begin seeking Him for **HIS WILL FOR YOUR LIFE**. Many times God will bring you to the point where you have to make difficult choices that will challenge some of the most treasured priorities and people in our lives.

> *"Draw nigh to God, and* **HE WILL DRAW NIGH TO YOU."**
> ***(James 4:8a)***

As you begin to seek Him, you will see that there will be things in your life that are not consistent with His plan that you will have to relinquish. The higher you go in God, the more things of the flesh and pleasing of men you will have to release. Jesus says:

IF YOU CAN GIVE IT UP, YOU CAN HAVE IT ALL !

6

IF YOU CAN GIVE IT UP, YOU CAN HAVE IT ALL

"He that findeth his life shall lose it: and
HE THAT LOSETH HIS LIFE *for my sake*
SHALL FIND IT."
(Matthew 10:39)

"Whosoever will come after me, let him deny himself, and take up his cross, and follow me."
(Mark 8:34b)

To lose your life means giving up the ambitions, desires, or personal plans that you have for your life in place of God's plan. It means I may want to be a radio disc jockey or high school principal, but God wants me to go into full-time ministry by being trained in ministry school. You may want to be the president of your ministerial alliance. There are people I know who had annual salaries of $50,000 – $60,000 that had to let it all go in order to follow God's plan for their lives. Now that's losing your life.

If you are going to fully and completely follow the Lord's plan for your life, somewhere along the way you will have to deny yourself of something that you would rather do. There is a cross to bear. We love being associated with Jesus when that fellowship brings the blessings and all the good things that He has to offer.

The Bible, however, also mentions the fellowship of His suffering:

> *"That I may know him, and the power of his resurrection, and the **FELLOWSHIP OF HIS SUFFERINGS**, being made conformable unto his death."*
> ***(Philippians 3:10)***

When speaking of taking up our cross, this is not a cross or suffering of our burdens, worries, bills, finances, habits, sickness, and pains. For years we have traditionally said that my sickness of diabetes is just the cross I've got to bear. In other words, I got to have these things. No, Jesus died for all of those things. He died for your sicknesses, your burdens, worries, your poverty and lack. He died for you to have peace of mind; He died for your sins, iniquities, and habits. These are not to be crosses for us because He bore those things over 2,000 years ago. All we need to do is appropriate what He did on the cross to our lives (See *Isaiah 53:5*).

There is, however, a cross that we must bear. The cross is anything you must bear, suffer, or deny yourself of in order to follow God's will for your life. It may mean giving up your plans, ambitions, that big salaried job, a position in an organization or denomination. It may mean losing the love, affection, respect, and admiration of people. It may mean being persecuted when people do not understand what God is doing in your life. When you decide to live godly and people separate themselves from you, that's a form of suffering. That's what you call losing your life – losing everything and sometimes everybody you have ever depended on to make you who you are. I found out that my life and most of my ministry was established on flesh, tradition, and people-pleasing. God was calling me to lose the life that had not been established totally by Him and find the life, path, and plan that He had for me.

When I made the decision to lose my life, when I made the decision to not try to save my life (self-preservation, reputation-saving, people-pleasing, comfort zone-keeping life), I found my life, the life God had predetermined for me. I found out that **IF YOU CAN GIVE IT ALL UP, YOU CAN HAVE IT ALL!**

THE SEARCH BEGINS

In early 1986, I was beginning to feel a pull in my spirit. I felt empty inside and knew that my spiritual life needed something else. I also did not feel that I was able to do anything to help better the lives of my people. I was preaching and doing what I knew to do. I had watched the preachers who were considered to be good. No one topped my brother. He could sing, preach, pray, and hoop; he could articulate and exegete a sermon like no other. His illustrations in his messages were classic.

So I figured if I did the same thing he did and preached the same way he did, I would make it and people would accept me. I borrowed some of his sermons and if I couldn't get it directly from him, I would get his tape and copy it off of a tape recorder. He taught me how to hoop. He taught me what to say. I learned from others how to say the things that brought the greatest reaction. Most preachers' thinking back then was, you really hadn't preached if you didn't get a certain amount of reaction or shouts from the people. We used to say, "you need some juice at the end of your sermon."

I had never experienced most of the things I said in my sermons. I only said what I heard others before me say. You had to say things that looked like you were deep, say some pretty little proverbs or run off a bunch of facts and sentences that made you look like you really knew something.

I even purchased sermons from other men who sold them and bought tapes of other ministers. I later found out that most of the messages preachers preached were to impress and be accepted among other preachers and to sound like we were theologically knowledgeable. We very rarely preached to help the people. Yes, we dealt a lot with their troubles, trials and burdens because we knew everybody in there was going through something. Of course, when you mention their trials, whatever they were going through at the time would cause an emotional reaction. My messages did not produce change. They got people through a day or two of their troubles, but without change of heart and life, no learning how to believe God.

When young preachers begin preaching, they search for someone they want to emulate. They end up reproducing what has been passed down. We learn to repeat someone else's experience with God and never know God for ourselves. We only use the Bible or read it for sermon material to get a text. Once the text is taken, we close the Bible.

A minister's pulpit ministry should be an outflow from his own spiritual life and growth. Whatever he is studying and meditating on for his own life should be ministered to that congregation, not just something he found to say; not just good sermons that we read or get out of books; not just what we hear other men teach and preach, but what God gives us by revelation of His Word. I did not know the Word of God. I did not have a prayer life.

SOUL WINNERS CONFERENCE 1985

It was Sis. Addie Love who shocked me into realizing that I didn't know as much as I thought I did. She had been a longtime faithful member of our church. I grew up in the church with her children. She was very instrumental in the change of our church in so many ways. She had been one of the church's main lead singers in the choir. During a Soul Winners Conference at our church in 1985, the guest minister, Rev. Harold Patton, presented the gospel to us in a way like we had never heard it before. Rather than give the traditional invitation, "Doors of the church are now open," he asked the question, "**IF YOU DIED TONIGHT, WOULD HEAVEN BE YOUR HOME?**"

For years, people were given the invitation to join the church, but they were never extended an invitation to receive Christ and deal with their hearts. You could ask people if they were saved and most church-going people would say, "yes." Why? Because people think being saved is being a church member, going to church, paying money, being baptized and other religious things. When you, however, ask a person "if he died tonight, where would he go?" it makes them take an introspective look at their lives, at that moment. You start thinking about your sins, where you are with God at that moment and not just sign up to be on the church's membership roll. Once people respond by saying, "No" or "I'm not sure," we would then share with them the plan of salvation for receiving Christ. This was very instrumental in the turn around of our church. You would be surprised at the number of people in the church who are not born again or are not sure about their salvation because church was presented to them and not Christ.

On the last night of the Soul Winners Conference, after Rev. Patton had presented the invitation, I was just about to close the service. At the last moment, Sis Love raised her hand and said, "Pastor don't close the service yet, I can't let this go any further. I got to get this right tonight. I want to know that I am going to Heaven." Rev. Patton proceeded to minister the plan of salvation to her. Heck, I didn't know how. Isn't that pitiful, preaching every week and telling people to come to Christ and don't know how to lead them to Christ. Oh, I could preach a sermon and invite you to sign up, but I didn't know how to get you to Heaven. This will shock you: **MOST PASTORS DON'T!**

That one event shook our church up. Long time members of the church who had heard her sing all those years were upset. They were really under conviction, but did not want to acknowledge it. Her honesty and fear of God touched the whole church. That following Sunday, because of what she did, I saw many others come to that altar to make sure they were saved or going to Heaven. From that point on, I never again gave an invitation to just join church, but to receive Christ.

SIS. LOVE AND THE HOLY GHOST

A year later, Sis. Love called me on the telephone and shared with me about her sister that lived in Ohio who told her about the Holy Ghost and speaking in tongues. She asked me how I felt about it. I gave her an answer through my traditional glasses and understanding. I told her it was not for everybody. Some do have that gift but not everyone. I said, "You already have the Holy Ghost." I gave the best "Baptist" answer I had. She seemingly accepted what I said and we hung up. However, there in my office I was shaken because when I opened to some of the passages she mentioned, I knew that it did not coincide with what our denomination taught, but it was in the Bible. It was also the first evidence of one of my members waking up to the truth. I knew I couldn't stay blind too long. It woke me up and I started to study for myself. Of course, a year after that I went to Tulsa. Later a few others mentioned learning things from Christian TV.

THE ROLE OF TELEVISION IN CRACKING TRADITION

I believe TV had a lot to do with cracking the traditional wall. Many people left their denominational churches in the 1970's and 1980's because of TV ministers such as Fred Price, John Osteen, Oral Roberts, Marilyn Hickey, Kenneth Copeland, Pat Robertson and many others. We were hearing truth right in our living rooms and no longer had to depend on Sunday services. We were hearing teaching on the Holy Spirit, tongues, healing, prosperity, faith, etc. and it exposed our traditions.

MY ABRAHAMIC EXPERIENCE

In 1987, once again, God challenged my faith in Him. Like Abraham, He required me to leave all to follow Him. He removed all the props that I had been leaning and depending on all of my life. Once you get rid of the props and you cease to depend upon them, all you have is God. You are forced to trust Him, which is why He will sometimes move you away from everything that is familiar, especially family. He wants you to Himself without the influence of others.

"Now the Lord had said unto Abram,
GET THEE OUT OF THY COUNTRY,
AND FROM THY KINDRED, AND FROM
THY FATHER'S HOUSE, *unto a land that I will shew thee: And I will make of thee a great nation, and I will bless thee, and make thy name great; and thou shalt be a blessing:"*

(Genesis 12:1-2)

God takes you out in order to take you into the place He has for you. I shall never forget channel surfing with my cable control box. One night, I stopped at the PTL network channel with Jim Bakker, right as the Holy Spirit was giving a word of prophecy. Of course, this was probably the year before the scandal. The words were as follows:

"The Spirit of the Lord would say to you: I have ruffled your nest. I have stirred you up. Do not be in despair, do not be discouraged for this is only a course correction. I have stirred you up; I have something higher for you and I will move you into the land and into the place that I have prepared for you since the beginning of time says the Spirit of the Lord."

At that moment, God confirmed the reason why I had become so restless and unhappy. It was Him that was shaking my world and causing the restlessness within me. He had ruffled my nest, my comfort zone. I had become a comfortable, established, settled pastor very early in my ministry.

I was the son of one of Memphis' most well-known black radio pastors, Rev. Jasper W. Williams, Sr., and the brother of one of the black Baptist denominations most prolific preachers, Jasper W. Williams, Jr. I inherited the family church that my father founded in 1944. He died in 1981. I became pastor that same year. Lane Avenue Baptist Church was one of Memphis' best churches. It was a well established church. At the time I became pastor, there was about 300-400 members on roll.

I walked into what some pastors called a "gold mine." I resigned from my full-time high school teaching job that year in order to pastor the church full-time. The church gave me a good salary, helped me to purchase a home, and bought a car for me. I inherited my father's radio broadcast. I immediately had everything that most pastors work a lifetime to get. I was made comfortable quickly. I had no reason in the world to leave all that I had, which takes me back to 1984 and the birth of our first child, Altronise.

WHEN GOD RUFFLES YOUR NEST
(COMFORT ZONE)

About six months after her birth, my wife, Sherrilyn and I noticed her scratching more and more. After going to the doctor, she was diagnosed with a serious skin disease called, atopic dermatitis. It was a skin condition that caused her to scratch until she bled. We would wake up in the mornings and her bed sheets were covered with blood. We tried several dermatologists, but no one could do her any good. As a matter of fact, one doctor took a skin analysis of her and said that the average for atopic dermatitis patients was 500 something or another. Our daughter rated 1500. Her problem was triple of whatever the norm was. We tried every oral medication and cream the doctors recommended. Nothing worked! God used this trial to bring me to my knees. No, I don't believe God did it, but I believe He used it at a time when my heart was humbled. We tend to hear God more or seek to hear Him when we are down. My nest was ruffled. I now had a reason to come out of my comfort zone.

Everything was comfortable until my daughter's disease. I had no reason to seek after God. Although as preachers, we are supposed to, when you have everything and your ministry is successful in the eyes of people, hey, you've got it made. My success proves that everything has got to be alright with God, so why do I need Him any more than what I already have.

With no hope from man, I started seeking God for her healing or some solution to her problem. My tradition did not teach that we could believe God for healing. We knew God could heal, but we were not taught that healing belongs to us or that we could believe Him to heal us.

HOW GOD PLACED PEOPLE AND BOOKS IN MY PATH

After I began seeking God and turning toward Him for help, this was the beginning of my transformation. I was now on the path of knowing Him in a way like I had never known Him before. The moment I began to draw near to Him, He began drawing near to me. Slowly, God began putting people in my path (some of whom I had known for years). Some were pastors who I did not know were Holy Ghost-filled. God began to put books, tapes, ministry magazines in my path. Some of these men shared with me about their experience with the Baptism with the Holy Ghost. Someone gave me some books by Kenneth Hagin on how to believe God for healing. Upon reading these books and seeing the simplicity of the Gospel in a way like I had never seen it before, those pamphlets and mini-books anointed by the Holy Ghost and not the wisdom of man, helped me to understand things that tradition and seminary confused me on. I knew I needed more. I saw from those books how much I didn't know. I read on the back of one of those books that Kenneth Hagin had a school which trained ministers in Tulsa, OK. From that point on, God made it stronger and stronger in my spirit to go. Yet, Satan, my flesh and my traditional mindsets caused me to struggle with this decision.

GOD WILL SPEAK TO YOU WHATEVER WAY HE CAN

As God began moving on my heart to go to school, one night He once again confirmed it through a prophecy that I accidentally saw on television. Since I didn't know how to listen to my spirit or how to hear God, God spoke to me where I was, through the TV. While channel surfing again, a man by the name of Bob Gass was ministering on the PTL network's Camp Meeting program in June of 1986. The following is the word God gave me by The Spirit:

> "I speak this by the Spirit of the Lord:
> There is a pastor watching me now and you are going through pure hell because God has told you exactly what to do, but those who love you most, you're having to climb above them. I believe the Word of the Lord is to get alone with God and what He's placed in your spirit He is going to make it stronger and stronger until you'll have the faith to rise above family, brethren and loved ones and go do the will of God. I give that to you in the name of Jesus. But you say Bob..."

He immediately went right back to teaching. God knows how to get your attention. I had not learned how to develop my spirit to become sensitive to the Holy Spirit, so God reached me and spoke to me where I was. I knew right away I was the pastor in that prophecy. I knew deep down in my spirit what God was saying, that I was trying to climb above those who I loved and felt loved me. The more I got with God, the stronger He made the desire to go.

THE INNER STRUGGLE TO GO TO SCHOOL

I saw four big problems in my mind that would hinder me from going. First of all, Tulsa was seven hours away from Memphis. As a full-time pastor, I wondered how I would be able to go to school and be in Memphis to pastor at the same time. To go to school meant possibly resigning from my pastorate. Secondly, I had a sick daughter. We felt more secure being in Memphis around family, friends, loved ones, and doctors who were familiar with her condition. I need to also add that we had applied and been approved for reservation residential space in Denver, Colorado at a Jewish Dermatology Medical Center, probably the best in the country. We would have to fly there and stay several weeks while they treated her. To get a reservation was a blessing because they had a waiting list of parents. It was the only hope we had at the time for our daughter who was now about three and a half years old. If we took the reservation, we would have missed enrolling in Rhema for the 1987-88 school year.

Thirdly, our whole family would have to move there. Our home would be left vacant. Rhema stressed the importance of married couples staying together, therefore spouses were required to come. If they did not consent, you could not enroll. This probably saved a lot of marriages, because there had been situations years before at Rhema where one spouse came, the other didn't. The student gets lonely and begins a companionship with a student of the opposite sex sitting near them in class. I am so grateful for that rule.

Finally, Rhema was not a traditional school conducive to Baptist theology. It was a Spirit-filled, tongue talking, healing-believing, faith, and prosperity-teaching school that was totally contrary to what I grew up believing. I knew my leaving the foundations of my family's religious belief system was going to ultimately cause an uproar. I say that because my family primarily ran and ruled the church. My mother was the underground pastor of the church. My oldest sister was like her first assistant. My brother, although not in name, was like the distant overseer of the family church. I loved, respected, and highly revered him. He was my idol as a preacher. I tried to emulate him like most preachers during that day. So there was a strong influence and quiet control that he had over my ministry. I never wanted to disappoint him. I always sought his approval, but never felt I got it.

During the first six years I just wore the title "pastor" and felt my role was to keep the church in the 'Williams' family. Therefore, as long as I kept things status quo or did the things that kept everything like they always were, everyone was happy. As long as my mother stayed in power to keep the church functioning in its old ways, everything was cool. No one expected me to be **THE** pastor.

The moment I began to pastor the church and move toward my destiny by going to school and ultimately resigning from the church, it caused a rift in the family. My family had their plan for my life, but God had another one for me. I knew this move would affect my relationship with my brother, as I had idolized him even into my early adult years. I also knew that what I was about to learn in Tulsa would probably shake up the church and possibly cause a split if they kept me on as pastor.

After several weeks and months of struggle and inner turmoil about whether I should go to Rhema or not, God began to confirm His Word to me that it was His will that I go. My biggest struggle was how I would make a living for my family in Tulsa. I had no other livelihood. I had not taught school in six years. Even if I tried to teach in Tulsa, I probably would not have Oklahoma certification and would have to go to school for some months in order to achieve that, and I needed income right away. So making that step of faith was not easy. I thought that once I told my deacons and church that I was going to school almost 400 miles away from home, that would be it. They would never go along with that. I prayed many times and asked the Lord to show me what to do.

In April 1987, the promptings in my spirit led me to go to Tulsa and spy out the land to see if God would speak to me there. I also wanted to get a feel for the city and the school. When I got into Tulsa, a peace came all over me. I could sense even then, even though I was not ready to admit it, that God's glory cloud had come to Tulsa. From that point on, neither Memphis nor the church felt quite the same.

THE LORD GIVES CONFIRMATION

At the motel we stayed in, I remember getting up one night about 1:00 or 2:00 a.m. I put my clothes on and went outside while my wife slept. There was an open grassy field in the back with a little tree stump. I sat on it and looked out into the starry sky. I began talking to the Lord asking Him to show me if He wanted me to come to Tulsa. I asked for outward confirmations. Then I remember saying, "Lord, if you want us here let someone say something to us about being here. Nobody here knows us, so if someone says something to us about being here, we will know that it is you speaking."

Three things happened. I went back into the room and went to sleep. The next day my wife and I went to a bookstore. I purchased about three books on the Baptism with the Holy Spirit. One book was entitled ***This Awakening Generation*** by the late John Osteen. Every Baptist pastor who wants something more should read this book. He talked about his struggle as a Baptist pastor and how he wanted more, but he was held captive by the traditions of men. God literally spoke to me and fired my spirit up just by reading this book.

One of the traditional, mental reasoning strongholds that I had in my mind from preachers, which kept me from making this step of faith, was that a pastor should never leave his church for anything. I knew if I told the church I was going to school and they didn't agree with it, I had to make a decision. If I decided to go on to school, that meant I had to leave the church pastorate. John Osteen's book, however, talked about how he had a sick daughter and sought the healing power of God even though he was a Baptist. That's right where I was, but the main thing was he left his church to pursue a business career because his ministry was not fruitful. Later, he went out on the mission field. Two to three years after that, God put him back in the same church. A confirmation to him and his church that God was changing it from a denominational church to a non-denominational one was depicted in the event of a rainstorm one night as they met for prayer. Their church sign, which was a three wood-planked sign; the top plank had "Lakewood," the middle plank had "Baptist" and the bottom plank had "Church" on it. When they went outside the next morning, the lightning had knocked the "Baptist" plank off. He saw it as a confirmation from God that they were no longer to be a Baptist Church.

I saw from this that just because you leave a particular work does not mean God will condemn you. I saw from this that there are times that God will even allow or call a pastor out. There are many pastors God is calling to do other things or maybe He never called them to pastor to begin with. They are miserable, nothing is going right, there is no fruit or growth, but they toil on because of a little measly security. They make their paycheck and church their source and not God.

The next thing occurred on the Sunday morning when we went to Rhema Church to experience their worship and the ministry of the Word of God. I must say that there was nothing spectacular that really impressed me. We sat a few rows from the door in which we entered. As the benediction was about to take place, my impatience said to my wife, "Let's beat the crowd and get to the bookstore," which was right outside in the lobby. I was closest to the aisle when I told my wife to come on, and I proceeded out of the door. I looked back and noticed that my wife was not with me. I waited a couple of minutes, and she still did not show up. I went back to the door, opened it and saw her hugging a white lady who was sitting behind us. I went on to the bookstore because knowing my wife and her love for mingling with people, she would be there for a while.

She came out of the church and spotted me in the bookstore. She brought this same lady over to me. My wife introduced her to me. Her name was Patsy. After the introduction, my wife said, "Patsy, tell my husband what you just told me." (I had told my wife earlier about the prayer that I prayed about someone speaking to us.) The lady went on to say, "When I saw the two of you come in, the Lord spoke to me to tell you that the two of you were supposed to be here in Tulsa at Rhema." My mouth flew open and my heart felt like it was about to explode. God had confirmed what I asked him to do.

Even the night before, on that Saturday, my wife went to the Wal-Mart store down the street from the motel. At the check-out register, she met a cashier whose husband was a first-year student at Rhema. She took down their number. I called him and he was so gracious. He was so on fire for the Lord and His Word that he was willing to go anywhere and share what he had learned. He and his wife came to the hotel that Saturday night around 10:30 or 11:00 p.m. We talked about three hours. He was so excited and he told me everything I needed to know about Rhema. God used Norman and Margaret Manning as two key persons to unlock the door to our destiny. We heard everything we needed to hear about the school and more. I had an orientation class on Rhema in my hotel room that night.

Yet, even after all of that, my mind still struggled with going. Before leaving Tulsa, my wife and I stopped by the office of the school's dean, Dean Moffett. We told him of our intentions of possibly coming to the school. I shared with him all of the various factors making it difficult to make the decision. He said, "If God has called you to come, He will take care of all your factors." He ended the conversation by saying, "God cannot begin to set things in motion for you until you make the decision. Once you make the decision, the struggle is over and God is free to move on your behalf. You are struggling because you have not decided and you are still betwixt and between." Yet, I still struggled for about another two months.

THE DECISION IS FINALLY MADE

I had become so restless, irritable and miserable that I did not want to even be at church anymore. I had no desire to even preach. My inner struggle and irritableness was even affecting my marriage. I had no peace because I was not obeying God.

Finally, in early July, I made the decision in my heart to go. I knew my first visible sign that the decision had been made was to tell my deacon board about my decision. I called an emergency meeting. Even before meeting with them, I felt the peace of God rise up inside me. The struggle was now over. I finally got to the point where I said to myself, "If I lose the church, house, salary, or approval of family, it doesn't matter anymore. I have got to obey God." I was tired of the struggle and wanted peace of mind.

Just as Dean Moffett had said, the moment I made the decision, God began to move. School started September 3rd that year. At the meeting with my deacons, Deacon Hosea Montgomery, Sr. got up and said, "Pastor, we sent your daddy to school. He would travel to Nashville and Mississippi to get his education. If we could send him and pay for his tuition, we can pay for yours. We don't want you to resign. Some of the ministers can carry on in your place." I told them that Tulsa was only a six or seven hour drive. I could drive home to preach on the weekend and drive back to Tulsa on Sunday evenings to be there for school on Monday morning.

They were all in agreement and even told me that they would continue to give me my present salary and added expense money to take care of my obligations in Tulsa. Satan had caused me a lot of unnecessary struggle. Once I obeyed God, He worked into the hearts of my deacons to help me to go to school. Remember, there are always blessings awaiting on the other side of your "**YES**" to the Lord. Obedience will cause you to eat the good of the land *(Isaiah 1:19)*. God prepared their hearts for me.

*"The kings' **HEART IS IN THE HAND OF THE LORD**, as the rivers of water: **HE TURNETH IT** whithersoever he will.*

(Proverbs 21:1)

The king represents anybody in authority. In this case, my deacons became the authority when it came to making this decision. This had to be God because the deacon board of a Baptist church should have said, "We want a pastor here full-time to counsel the people, visit the sick, oversee the church, etc." But for some reason they saw the vision. It had to be God's divine influence upon their hearts. They also really didn't understand the kind of school to which I was going.

OFF TO TULSA

At that point we were off to Tulsa. My wife and I went back to Tulsa in late July to find an apartment, and she wanted to apply for a job. A friend of mine, Ronald Montgomery (Bro. Montgomery's son, who I grew up with in the church), told us to have her to apply at American Airlines. American Airlines is to Tulsa what FedEx is to Memphis (Tulsa's biggest employer). His wife worked for American Airlines in Dallas. This would get us some flight benefits.

My wife got the job. I drove to Memphis and back to Tulsa every weekend for five months to preach to my people. Every now and then, maybe once a month I would stay home and rest. After an initial probationary period of a few months, we were able to use my wife's flight benefits and fly every weekend for only $10 or $15 round trip.

*"Now unto him that is able **TO DO EXCEEDING ABUNDANTLY ABOVE ALL THAT WE ASK OR THINK,** according to the power that worketh in us."*
(Ephesians 3:20)

Not only that, but God took care of my other problem with my first born, Altronise. Because of our obedience to follow Him first, rather than seek our own way for finding a remedy, God blessed us. We went to Oral Roberts Hospital, found a saved dermatologist by the name of Dr. Terrance Carey. The first medication that he recommended was called E.E.S. 200 along with a topical skin cream. For the first time in almost three years we found something that stopped the itching and controlled the problem. In Memphis, we went to several doctors and used everything they recommended, but nothing worked until we got in the perfect will of God in Tulsa.

Although, the medication did not take the problem away, it controlled the problem and gave me the peace I needed to go to school. In 1990 after returning home from Tulsa, my daughter would need a deliverance in order to see healing.

7

THE SCHOOL OF FAMILY

Many of God's greatest men had to contend with family problems while on the way to fulfilling their destiny.

- Abel- *Genesis 4:1-8*
- Jacob - *Genesis 27:41*
- Joseph - *Genesis 37:3,4,18-23*
- Moses - *Numbers 12:1-16*
- David - *1 Samuel 17:28*
- Jesus - *Mark 6:3-4; Matthew 12:46-50; John 2:1-4*

To follow the Lord can sometimes mean a break from your family, especially if your family members are unsaved, unchurched, unspiritual, untrained in the Word of God, or in my case preserving denominational roots. If you are going to obey God, it's going to cost you something, possibly the love, affection and closeness of your family. The Bible confirms this over and over. When you make the decision to follow the Lord fully, the first class you must take is Family 101. Abraham's first course was leaving family *(Genesis 12:1-2)*.

Family is usually the closest thing to you. Your beliefs and values are formed by your family. There are expectations developed by family for your life. There is a family pride and reputation that is established. You are sometimes taught that family is first. In some cases, people are taught that the family comes before a spouse; if it is not said, it is usually implied. You must always be there for family, "we must be able to depend on you." That's why breaking the controlling powers of your family will not be easy.

There are many Christians who cannot do all that God has called them to do because they are controlled by the desire of family. I see many who are even controlled by loved ones who have been dead for years. They make allegiances to a grandmother that they will get their master's degree, but God may be calling them into the ministry. Our duty and obligation in life is not to please family.

> *"Let us hear the conclusion of the whole matter:*
> ***FEAR GOD AND KEEP HIS COMMANDMENTS:***
> ***FOR THIS IS THE WHOLE DUTY OF MAN."***
>
> *(Ecclesiastes 12:13)*

CAN'T MAKE THE BREAK WITHOUT KNOWLEDGE

I could not make that break from family until I had some knowledge of God's will and/or Word. Once I received some promises from the Word, I received the assurance and confidence that I needed to step out. I might also add that making the break from family does not mean ignoring them, staying away from them or not having anything to do with them. This is what the cults do. That's not of God. It means not allowing family to stop you from following God's will for your life. Even though misunderstanding, ostracization, bitter feelings or offenses may come, we are commanded by God to always walk in love *(Hebrews 13:1)*.

LOSING IT ALL FOR HIS SAKE

Like the Apostle Paul, I had to come to the point where:

"I COUNT EVERYTHING AS LOSS compared to the possession of the priceless privilege - the overwhelming preciousness, the surpassing worth and supreme advantage - of knowing Christ Jesus my Lord, and of progressively becoming more deeply and intimately acquainted with Him, of perceiving and recognizing and understanding Him more fully and clearly. FOR HIS SAKE, I HAVE LOST EVERYTHING and consider it all to be mere rubbish (refuse, dregs), in order that I may win (gain) Christ, the Anointed One."

(Philippians 3:8 – Amplified)

Once you can count everything and everybody in your life that means something to you as loss in exchange for acquiring more intimate knowledge of Christ, then God is ready to do a work in your life. Once you get hungry for God, nothing else in this world really matters.

Many times, depending on the call and purpose of your life, God will pull you away from any and everything that will influence you from walking with Him. As I have already stated, Abraham had to be pulled away from all of his family traditions and idolatrous customs. God had to put him in a position where he could hear Him and learn to trust Him. Do not be surprised when God makes you the outcast of your family or the "**BLACK SHEEP**" in their eyes.

*"**GOD SETTETH THE SOLITARY IN FAMILIES:**
he bringeth out those which are bound
with chains: ..."*

(Psalm 68:6)

By placing you in a solitary position from your family, He will speak to you, teach you and lead you to bring your family and others out of bondage. I believe God has at least one in every family that represents a remnant of His people. His intent is to do for you what He did for Abraham:

*"... and thou shalt **BE A BLESSING**"*
(Genesis 12:2)

God may not always move you geographically from your family. Sometimes it is the emotionally, dependent attachments that He separates. He will call upon you, however, to be the one in the family that seems to not fit into the family mold. Like Joseph, He may use you to deliver your family from its' bondages. In Joseph's case, his family did not see who he was. They misunderstood him and did not recognize the anointing and call upon his life. This can happen because all family can see sometimes is who you have always been: 'Pooky', 'June Bug', 'Me-Me', 'Butch', and 'Beanhead' or whatever your family identity nickname was.

God needs your life to be an example and light to your family that will pull them out of sin or religious tradition. No matter how your family persecutes you and talks against you because of your walk with God, when they get desperate in life's crisis, guess who they will call on to get a prayer through? Yes, you.

I did not totally understand the separation from family back then. Looking back on everything, however, I had to go through it to break the apron strings and attachments and be able to follow the Lord with no control or influence by family. I could not have done it without knowledge of God's Word. Knowing what God said gave the grace (divine influence upon the heart; favor, ability, peace and strength) to rise above family dependence.

*"**GRACE AND PEACE BE MULTIPLIED** unto you **THROUGH THE KNOWLEDGE OF GOD**, and of Jesus our Lord."*

(2 Peter 1:2)

Grace (or God's favor) and peace is multiplied or increased when you have knowledge of God and of Jesus our Lord. That's why if you are not being fed the Word of God where you are going to church, you will never see God's favor and peace increased in your life.

"According as his divine power hath ***GIVEN UNTO US ALL THINGS THAT PERTAIN UNTO LIFE*** *and godliness,* ***THROUGH*** *the* ***KNOWLEDGE*** *of him ..."*
(2 Peter 1:3)

God has given us everything we need to live life and live it through godliness. It comes, however, through having knowledge. If you are not being taught that it is the will of God for you to have favor, peace, blessings, success, power, prosperity, healing, deliverance, victory over trials, and abundance, then you are not being properly fed the Word of God. If you are not being taught to believe God, or to trust Him by faith; if you are not being taught that you have authority over the devil; if you are not being taught who you are in Christ: the righteousness of God, more than a conqueror, an overcomer, or a victorious Christian, then you will never be able to rise above the circumstances of life. You will always have to live and depend on others and be in fear of them if they won't come through for you *(Psalm 118:6)*.

WILL IT BE GOD OR FAMILY?

Many of you are saying, "I'm empty inside. I'm hungry for God. I need more than what I am getting." You may have even been to the church you would like to join in order to have that need met. But that family pull of loyalty is holding you to your traditional church. If you decide to leave, you know that it will ultimately affect your relationship with your family. Jesus lets us know the price we will have to pay to follow Him when it comes to family.

"Think not that I am come to send peace on earth: **I CAME NOT TO SEND PEACE BUT A SWORD.** *For I am come to set a man at variance (at odds) against his father, and the daughter against her mother, and the daughter-in-law against her mother-in-law.*
(Matthew 10:34-35)

Do not get the wrong impression about this passage of scripture. Jesus did not come to purposely destroy our family relationships and keep us from having peace. Keep in mind He is called the Prince of Peace *(Isaiah 9:6)*. He died for our peace *(Isaiah 53:5)*, and then said He would leave us His peace *(John 14:27)*. He tells us to follow peace, seek peace, and that the peacemaker is blessed *(Hebrews 12:14; Matthew 5:8)*. Jesus is saying that His presence in a world contrary to the ways of God will ultimately cause division in the earth and can affect the peace of family relationships.

When one or more members of a family desire to follow God and His Word, will, or ways, it's going to bring division. If your unsaved or carnal family is not ready to change and give their lives to God, they will not feel comfortable with your godly lifestyle. Your walk with God will bring light to their darkness and put pressure on them when they don't want to change.

"And this is the condemnation, that light is come into the world, and men loved darkness rather than light, because their deeds were evil. **FOR EVERY ONE THAT DOETH EVIL HATETH THE LIGHT, NEITHER COMETH TO THE LIGHT, LEST HIS DEEDS SHOULD BE REPROVED** *(or exposed).*

(John 3:19-20)

FAMILY PERSECUTION

We know this is the case with unsaved or ungodly families, even in church-going traditional families, who go to church on Sunday, sing in the choir, give a little money, serve in a certain high position as assurance that all is right with God. Yet, a little sin on the side is alright. I never had any biblical debates with my family concerning Pentecostal issues. I have counseled, however, many members who have joined my church. They told me when they went home talking about being filled with the Holy Ghost, speaking in tongues, laying on of hands for healing, discerning Satan, and living a holy or godly life, they were not ready for family persecution *(John 15:20)*. They thought everybody would be excited with their new knowledge of God's Word and His blessing. No, that will not always happen because it means change and hearts being exposed, and their families did not want their sins exposed.

There is a big difference in Christianity and "Churchanity". Most of us have only known church and not Christ. When you begin to pursue the Christ and not the church only, you can expect ostracization and ridicule from family or those close to you. Most churchgoers have yet to find out what true Christianity really is. Church folk only want God to keep them out of hell; meet their needs, and get them delivered from their trials when they get in trouble. That is the extent of most church going folk's relationship with God. They know nothing about seeking Him, living godly for Him, living by faith, believing and receiving His Word, or finding God's purpose for their lives. All they know is "having church."

A great mistake that families make is equating the church with God. So many people, when they are ready to make that step to another church, have to hear parents or siblings say, "You been in this church all your life; it's wrong for you to leave. You grew up in here." People make their loyalties to a particular local congregation, and that's wrong. Your loyalty is to Jesus Christ. As long as you stay with Him, you will always be alright with your Heavenly Father. To say that you are wrong for leaving a particular church is to say that that church must be the only church that has God in it. No, your allegiance should be to God and not necessarily a particular congregation, unless you know God has placed you there and told you not to leave. This can sometimes cause family to be very disappointed in you.

*"And a man's **FOES (ENEMIES)** shall be they of **HIS HOUSEHOLD"***

(Matthew 10:36)

Family can become your adversary when it comes to God and His presence in your life. There will come a day when you might have to make that choice between family and God. That one choice could determine your destiny.

*"He that loveth father or mother more than me is **NOT WORTHY OF ME:** and he that loveth son or daughter more than me is **NOT WORTHY OF ME.***

(Matthew 10:37)

When you allow the control and desires of loved ones to become priority over your quest to know the Lord, God says you are not worthy of Him. If your family says to you, "We are not going to have anything to do with you, if you go to that church over there, that speaking in tongues, praising and dancing church," you have got a choice to make at that moment. You are either going, however, with family and miss the blessings, plans, and purposes of God for your life, or go with God and ultimately help lead your family to their destiny. I would not want to have to stand before God on Judgment Day and hear Him say I was not worthy of Him.

LOYALTY TO DENOMINATIONS AND NOT GOD

God is not concerned about your family loyalties and sentimental feelings. Staying in a church just because you grew up there or three to four generations of family members went there or 'This is where my parents were married or funeralized;' 'This is where all of my family goes to church;' 'This is the only denomination that our family has been a part of'; 'I been Baptist born, Baptist bred, and when I die I'll be a Baptist dead' does not move God.

People are more denominationally-conscious than they are God-conscious. People have made the denomination their god. Many are actually afraid to venture outside of their denomination. We are indoctrinated to believe that the denomination of my family is where I must stay. "If it was alright for momma-nem, who I know wouldn't lie to me, it's alright for me." That's where we get stuck in our denominations, by family loyalty. That's why God had to place scriptures throughout the Bible to warn His people of making family loyalty a priority over loyalty to Him *(Luke 14:26)*.

If you were to ask most people why they are Baptist, Methodist, or whatever, they could not tell you why, other than their family loyalty. Most people can't even tell you what their denomination believes. They have never checked. They have never compared their church doctrinal statement of beliefs with the Word of God to even know if it is consistent with scripture. It's totally out of family loyalty.

For African-American Christians, their denominational loyalties go all the way back to the slave plantations. Most of your plantation slave owners were either Baptist or Methodist. The denominational identity of the plantation owner would be the slave's place of worship. If the plantation slave owner was Baptist, he would carry his slaves with him to church to sit in the balcony of his Baptist church on Sunday morning. This is how we got our church identity, because "if it was good enough for 'Massa Moe', it's good enough for us." This usually lasts for many generations thereafter, until someone wakes up.

The first slave generation begins to trust in the slave master's church and now the next generation does the same thing. Finally, when blacks were able to form their own churches, they kept the denominational name they were familiar with. So for generations and generations, we stay in the same denomination.

Again, God is not concerned about the things we make important or use as excuses as to why we can't move on to another church. Some people stay at a church because they are in a high position. They have worked their way to the top and have people that they influence. That's difficult for many people to give up. We are afraid if we go to another church, we may not ever get back to the top again. God's concern is that you learn how to be conformed to the image of Christ *(Romans 8:29)*. When people tell me that they are confused about whether or not they should leave a church, my question to them has always been, "Do you feel that you are becoming more like Christ where you are?" "Do you sense you are understanding God more by the ministry of your pastor?"

HOW TO FIND A GOD-KIND OF PASTOR

God gives the acid test as to whether or not you have the right church and pastor. How do I know the pastors according to God's own heart?

> *"And I will give you **PASTORS** according to mine heart, **WHICH SHALL FEED YOU** with **KNOWLEDGE** and **UNDERSTANDING**."*
>
> *(Jeremiah 3:15)*

If you are not understanding the ways of God, His truths and principles are not being taught. If all you hear are stories like David and Goliath, rhymes, poetry and pretty phrases, social messages, the rules of the denomination, sermons that make you feel good emotionally, sermons that control you and keep you in fear and condemnation or sermons that tend to teach you to overlook sin; if you feel as though you are on spiritual milk and not meat, you may need to think and pray again about your church. I'm alright about a little hooping, but make sure you feed me something to live by.

EXCUSES TO STAY IN TRADITION

I have talked with people who knew they were in the wrong church and not being fed. Their way of giving themselves an excuse to stay was, "Some of us need to stay back here to pray that the pastor would change." My response is, "You can pray for the pastor to change while you are at another church that's going to feed you." You don't have to stay at the church in order to pray for the pastor. Also, no one's prayer has the ability to control the will of another person. If that pastor is happy where he is and he does not have a desire to change, you may never see any growth in Christ and you'll be praying for decades.

Some people feel like they have a little more knowledge than the pastor, and it is their job to stay and see to it that others in the church learn more. That's why they need to stay and hold on to their Sunday school class. They begin to get the Messiah syndrome, "I am the one God is going to use to change this. It's up to me. The people need me."

All of these are excuses to hold on to power, prestige, and family affection. God placed that pastor over that flock, not you. Only he can give an account to God for it *(Hebrews 13:17; Proverbs 27:23; Acts 20:28; 1 Peter 5:2)*. You are making a serious mistake if you think that God is going to use you to change a church that He has given to another man to oversee, and you are in serious rebellion if you come in and teach something contrary to the teachings of your pastor. God will honor his authority over that church even if he isn't teaching what you think he should be teaching. That man will have to stand before God for his ministry *(Romans 14:1-10)*. Your doing this could be interfering with the timing of God. God could be working in his heart, but your untimely move could start a rebellion in the church that could hinder or prolong God from moving.

As it relates to the people, each individual must make their own decision as to who will feed them. I don't care if a pastor never taught the Bible or truth in 40 years of ministry, everything cannot be blamed on him. Once people become hungry for God, then they will know that they need more and will make the necessary decisions concerning their spiritual lives. That's why it is not up to you to take responsibility for the people. People who think that way really desire their own following *(Acts 20:29-30)*, which is why they want to stay and keep their position. When you really want God and more of Him and His Word, you will leave it all and count it all loss to find Him; position, prestige, and power, don't matter. Maybe family needs you to stay in order to help them keep their influence in the church. When you want God, you will leave it and drop it all to find Him.

JESUS AND HIS FAMILY

Even Jesus' family did not receive Him as He set out to obey the call of God upon His life.

> *"Is not this the carpenter, the son of Mary, the brother of James, Joses, and of Judah, and Simon? And are not his sisters here with us? And they were offended at him. But Jesus said unto them,* **A PROPHET IS NOT WITHOUT HONOUR, BUT IN HIS OWN COUNTRY, AND AMONG HIS OWN KIN, AND IN HIS OWN HOUSE.**
>
> *(Mark 6:3-4)*

Jesus received persecution and rejection from his own family and kin, who did not understand or recognize who He was. Did Jesus, however, allow the demands and control of family to become priority over the will of God? Remember, He is our example *(1 Peter 2:21)*. Let's look at an episode in His life to see how He handled family and who was priority, family or God. (This was one of the passages of scripture that helped me to break free.)

> *"While he yet talked to the people, behold,* **HIS MOTHER AND HIS BRETHREN STOOD WITHOUT, DESIRING TO SPEAK WITH HIM.** *Then one said unto him, Behold, thy mother and thy brethren stand without, desiring to speak with thee."*
> ***(Matthew 12:46-47)***

While Jesus was ministering to the people one day, His family sent for Him to come out and speak with them. They wanted Him to stop preaching the Word of God to the people and come see what they wanted. I love His response to the one who brought Him the message:

> *"But he answered and said unto him that told him,* **WHO IS MY MOTHER? AND WHO ARE MY BRETHREN? AND HE STRETCHED FORTH HIS HAND TOWARD HIS DISCIPLES,** *and said,* **BEHOLD MY MOTHER AND MY BRETHREN!"**
> ***(Matthew 12:48-49)***

Allow me to paraphrase what Jesus said in these two verses. "Do you want to know who my real mother and brethren are? With his hands pointing toward the people, these people that you see sitting in front of me. They are my real mother and brethren." Why would Jesus say that?

> *"For* **WHOSOEVER SHALL DO THE WILL OF MY FATHER,** *which is in heaven,* **THE SAME IS MY BROTHER, AND SISTER, AND MOTHER."**
> ***(Matthew 12:50)***

Jesus placed more priority on His spiritual family, than He did His natural family. His disciples loved God enough to sit at His feet and hear the words of God. Therefore, at that moment they were doing the will of God. His natural family was not. Rather than come in and hear the Word of God, they stayed outside and beckoned for Him to stop doing God's will and come see what they wanted. They felt family loyalty should supersede His commitment to God and His call, which is the same thing your family asks you to do.

The bottom line is doing the will of God. Family may turn their backs on you and want to separate themselves from you, but if you want to be in the will of God and have the blessings of God upon your life, you must do and obey the will of God for your life.

*"If ye be willing and **OBEDIENT, YE SHALL EAT THE GOOD OF THE LAND.**"*
(Isaiah 1:19)

*"If they **OBEY** and serve him, they shall **SPEND THEIR DAYS IN PROSPERITY AND THEIR YEARS IN PLEASURES.** But if they obey not, they shall perish by the sword, and they shall die without knowledge."*
(Job 36:11-12)

You will find that once you find the Lord, your greatest need and desire is to connect with others who love the Lord. Although, you love your family and always will, you feel a greater connection with those who also have a desire to follow the will of God. Why? Because they understand the things that are going on inside you when family cannot. You have things in common. When you begin to move into spiritual things, family, loved ones, and others who do not understand and only see things in the natural, will think you are foolish.

*"But the **NATURAL MAN RECEIVETH NOT THE THINGS OF THE SPIRIT OF GOD: FOR THEY ARE FOOLISHNESS** unto him: neither can he know them, because they are spiritually discerned."*

(1 Corinthians 2:14)

God blesses you to find out some great things that you are excited about, and you want family and others to be blessed. You hear about tongues and how it can assist you in prayer; how we can prosper, be healed and delivered. You share it with natural-minded family members and friends, and they don't want to hear it. They will call you crazy and foolish. Why? Because their hearts and minds have not been opened to spiritual things.

*"[That is] because the mind of the flesh [with its carnal thoughts and purposes] is hostile to God, for it does not submit itself to God's Law; indeed it cannot. **SO THEN THOSE WHO ARE LIVING THE LIFE OF THE FLESH** [catering to the appetites and impulses of their carnal nature] **CANNOT PLEASE OR SATISFY GOD, OR BE ACCEPTABLE TO HIM."***

(Romans 8:7-8 – Amplified)

That's why Jesus placed more emphasis on your spiritual family, than He did your natural family. They understand the will of God. Jesus said that those who do the will of God are my real family. If your family fails to do the will of God, God will fill that void in your life by giving you a family of the spirit. When I lost my natural, blood family, God gave me people like Bishop Leroy Bailey of First Cathedral in Hartford, CT, who believed in the things I had learned. He became like a brother to me. He had carried his church through a transition years earlier and called me because he knew what I was going through.

The world says, "Blood is thicker than water." In other words, people of the same blood are supposed to have a closer relationship than anyone else. Jesus is saying, however, spirit is thicker and greater than blood, or spiritual blood is thicker than natural blood.

8

GOING AND NOT KNOWING

In September of 1988, I was in my second and last year of school at Rhema. I began to get strong impulses to resign from the church. My original desire and intent was to move back to Memphis after completing school. I did not understand why I was feeling that way. Yet, I kept hearing in my spirit it was time to leave.

I must admit being in Tulsa, away from Memphis was the greatest time of our lives. We felt the peace of God. We knew the cloud was definitely over Tulsa for us at that time. You can also tell when the cloud moves, because things don't go as well and there is no real peace. This happened to us later.

I began to seek God for more confirmation of what I was getting in my spirit. When I am not sure that I am hearing from God correctly, there is a biblical principle that I use to help give me guidance:

*"This is the third time I am coming to you.
In the mouth of **TWO OR THREE WITNESSES**
shall every word be established.*

(2 Corinthians 13:1)

I asked God for at least two or three confirmations to let me know that it was Him. Once again, God came through and gave me what I asked of Him. In September of that year (the same month), R.W. Shambach came to the ORU Mabee

Center. After preaching, he called for people who were sensing God telling them to step out and obey Him in something, but you are afraid. I immediately went down. Yet, it was still not enough.

Secondly, my best friend, Pastor Bobby Coney, who knew about my struggles in following the Lord, sent me a tape series by Chuck Swindoll on Abraham. The main tape he wanted me to hear was **'GOING AND NOT KNOWING.'** I remember Thanksgiving of that year, my wife and I got a babysitter for our two children and went to a hotel to spend some quality time with each other. While there, we listened to this tape. Every word was for me. It was like God was in that room speaking to me, Himself. That tape was key to strengthening my inner man with faith to make the step. He said, "You have to go and not know where it will lead."

I did not mind going; I just wanted to know where I was going. I wanted everything to be in place before I made my step. He told of how God called Abraham to leave family and go to a place where He would show him *(Genesis 12:1)*. He told Abraham to take Isaac and offer him as a sacrifice *(Genesis 22:2)*. God told him what land to go to, but He did not tell him which mountain. There was no need to tell him which mountain until he started out in obedience toward the land of Moriah.

I have found out over the years that God will not show you the full picture of your life at one time. He gives it to you in steps. One step of obedience determines whether or not God will give you the next step. There have been times I felt my life had become spiritually stagnated, and I wasn't hearing from God. I found out that the reason was I had not obeyed the last thing God told me to do. When I go back and obey the last thing He told me, I usually get the next step. Your next step depends on you making the previous one.

If God showed us every step we had to take ahead of time or everything we would have to go through on the path of reaching our destiny, we would probably say "No thank you Lord; I'll just stay in my traditions." Each step of obedience, however, builds your faith and prepares you for the next one. That's why God has to give you one step at a time. If I had known about the persecution, loss of family affection, abandonment of friends, fellow preachers, ministry opportunities that I lost, being misunderstood, losing members that I loved, betrayal, rejection, people misjudging your motives, loneliness, church strife and confusion, loss of salary, savings account, loss of pastorate, and other things that I had to endure while on my way to my destiny, I would have never gone to Tulsa. I would have told God, "No thank you." I'm so glad He didn't show me everything.

The third and final confirmation came while in my 'Submission and Authority' class at Rhema, taught by Keith Moore. He gave a prophetic word to the entire class. That day I knew God was saying it's time to go. He said:

> "Eighty-eight would be great but eighty-nine would be transition time...And ninety would be mighty...I think I can already see a lot of the transition; we're not quite in eighty-nine yet, but things are already beginning to shift. I looked up the definition of transition. It means to move from one place to another; from one responsibility; one capacity; its change. But many times in getting to the place God has for you, you will go through transition. And one thing that I do want you to understand, is that, it will take faith through a transition because a lot of times you are moving out of something you are familiar with and something that you are comfortable with and you are moving out into the unknown. Often times, the grace and anointing that was on you to do a job that you so enjoyed begins to lift from you and may come on somebody else; and maybe they do a better job at it than you could...You just need to have enough faith to know that God's got something else for me that will be better for

me. But you have got to turn loose of this 'NOT KNOWING WHERE YOU ARE GOING.' And that takes faith. When you are in the middle of a transition, don't think, PRAY...You sit around and try to think and figure out what's going on. You are going to concoct your own ideas and your own plans and what you think is going on, misapply, misinterpret, and misunderstand. No, when there is transition, you don't know what's going on, find God by praying in tongues, get by yourself, get your mind quiet and pray. Don't think – pray. If you catch yourself sitting around thinking: what's going on – don't do that. Get to praying, pray about it."

I was as good as gone. I began formulating my letter of resignation to the church in my mind that day. God had confirmed my next move.

SHOW ME FIRST, THEN I'LL STEP

Even with all that, I struggled with questions to God like, "How will I make it? How will I take care of my family?" The only thing I've ever done is pastor or teach school. How will I take care of these two notes I've got to pay? I had my home mortgage note in Memphis and my apartment note in Tulsa, which totaled about $935. Once I resign, I no longer have that income.

So I began to pray, "Lord, I'm ready to step out and transition to wherever you want me to go. I'm ready to resign, but how are you going to replace my income? I've got a wife and two children. I will resign when my needs are met."

I knew the first thing I had to do was find an apartment with a low monthly note. November of 1988, my wife and I were invited to a fellow Rhema student's house for dinner. He and his wife lived in a nice two-story, two-bedroom townhouse. The rooms were so nice and spacious. When I made the decision that I was going to let the church go, my mind went back to Willie's townhouse. He told me that he was paying only $50.00 a month. They were remodeled Section 8 apartments and townhomes. He told us that he knew the apartment manager very well and would talk to him for us.

He later called and told us to go over and speak with the manager. We went and he told us that it was not his decision. The Oklahoma State Housing Authority accepted applications and would authorize tenants for occupancy. We called and found out that there was a three-year waiting list. That's right, three years.

GOD SAYS, STEP FIRST THEN I'LL SHOW YOU

I asked God what happened. I can't wait three years. Deep in my spirit I heard a voice say, "You have not trusted me. **UNTIL YOU OBEY ME AND RESIGN FIRST, I CANNOT MOVE ON YOUR BEHALF.** Without faith, it is impossible to please God. It was frightening to go and resign knowing I had all of this indebtedness in Memphis and Tulsa. I knew God had, however, spoken and I had to obey. I gave the church my letter of resignation in January of 1989. Three days after the Sunday I did that, we called the Oklahoma State Housing Authority again. A friendly Christian woman answered the telephone and told us there was a vacancy in the apartments that we could get. I shouted! I knew God was sanctioning the move.

After evaluating our income, they charged us only $29 a month. Upon re-evaluating our application, they found out that we did not have to pay anything. God gave us an apartment for free. I used my savings to take care of the note and expenses in Memphis. **GOD IS GOOD.**

EL SHADDAI SHOWS UP

We lived out of our savings for several months thereafter. We had to return one of our cars back to Memphis because it was leased. We were down to one car and desperately needed two. The Internal Revenue Service called and said we owed them about $1,100. These two items would have devastated our savings account.

One day after praying and believing God for finances, I was sitting on the floor of our apartment looking at the low balance of my checkbook as I made out the bills. All of a sudden, I heard a voice say, "Look in the garbage can. The mail you threw away has something in it." The day before, I threw away a sheet concerning an investment plan that I had back in Memphis. I remembered, however, pulling the investment down and closing it before I left for Tulsa. When I read the sheet and saw the figures, I called my secretary, Sandra Cox, to see what it meant. Come to find out I had over $2,000 still left in stocks. This would have paid off IRS and helped to buy a used car. We applied for the dividend check and received it in 4-5 days. That in itself was a miracle because this process usually takes weeks.

We purchased our car and then disputed IRS's claim, which they dismissed. **GOD IS GOOD. EL SHADDAI IS MORE THAN ENOUGH.** Jehovah Jireh (The Lord our Provider) came through again. We saw God do several miracles like this, all because of our pursuit of His Word. We saw that we could depend on and trust in Him, even after all others had forsaken us.

During this time we went to a service at Victory Christian Center. On this day, John Avanzini ministered on sowing and reaping. He told of how he sowed and gave away a car and someone gave him a brand new car and how his wife gave away a coat and someone gave her a new mink coat. When the offering time came up, my checkbook register showed only $500, and I heard the Spirit tell me to give half of it. I like to have had a fit, but I obeyed. It was the week after this, that the $2,000 came and IRS dismissed their claim.

THE FEAR OF LIFE AND MAN IS BROKEN

Our dependence on man was over. Our fear of man and what he could do to us or not do for us was now broken. We found out that God was really real. He was no longer just somebody we heard about in sermons, from parents, or sung about. He was real; He was there! I knew I could go anywhere now and make it! This was part of God's reason for causing me to leave it all. I had to learn to find Him and trust Him.

> *"THE LORD IS ON MY SIDE; I WILL NOT FEAR:*
> *what can man do unto me?*
> *(Psalm 118:6)*

> *"...I will never leave thee, nor forsake*
> *thee. So that we may boldly say, The*
> *Lord is my helper, AND I WILL NOT*
> *FEAR WHAT MAN SHALL DO UNTO ME."*
>
> *(Hebrews 13:5-6)*

You might be asking what does all of this have to do with tradition? The purpose of this is to show you that if you are required by God to leave or make special sacrifices in your pursuit of Him, He is obligated to take care of you. When you go out on a limb to trust God like that, He has to come through for you. You may have to go out of town, leave the house and all dependence on family and friends, but He will meet your every need.

> *"And Jesus answered and said, Verily I say*
> *unto you, There is no man **THAT HATH***
> ***LEFT HOUSE OR BRETHREN**, or **SISTERS**,*
> *or **FATHER**, or **MOTHER**, or **WIFE**,*
> *or **CHILDREN**, or **LANDS**, **FOR MY SAKE***
> ***AND THE GOSPEL'S**, But he shall **RECEIVE***
> ***AN HUNDREDFOLD NOW IN THIS***
> ***TIME**, houses, and brethren, and sisters,*
> *and mothers, and children, and lands,*
> ***WITH PERSECUTIONS**; and in the*
> *world to come eternal life.*
>
> *(Mark 10:29-30)*

No other scripture helped me to break the influence and control of family along with the fear of letting go of things, like this scripture. Jesus said: there is no man that has left all for me that I won't give him back one hundred percent of what he lost. He presents the three main concerns that people will have when faced with that decision - family, people, and material things. He is saying any man, not just the Jews, not just the people of His day, not just white folks, but any man that will leave it all for the sake of the Gospel (the Word), will receive a hundredfold return, not only in the future life, but now, in this time that we are living in (on earth). However, when the blessings of God are on your life, it will breed jealousy and persecution.

9

YOU MUST DEAL WITH PERSECUTION

The Bible says: when you make the decision to live godly or live according to the ways of God, you will suffer persecution *(2 Timothy 3:12)*. To persecute means to press down on or to put pressure on.

Believe me, I have lived this message. This book is not birthed out of something I read or someone else's testimony. I have lived through every bit of it. I heard someone say, "Before I hear your message, show me your wounds. I want to know that you have been through something." As the old folk used to say, "I have been buked and scorned, talked about sho as you born."

When I began to deviate from Baptist tradition, I was called everything, but a child of God. I heard people say things like, "I know his daddy is turning over in his grave." "He's just messing up his daddy's church." "I bet his brother doesn't like it." "He went to Tulsa and let them white folks mess him up." "Don't go over to A. R.'s church because his doctrine isn't sound." "He's been out there at Oral Roberts school and he came back crazy."

First of all, it wasn't Oral Roberts, it was Kenneth Hagin. Secondly, when you have been in tradition so long, lies sound like the truth and the truth sounds like lies. Tradition can only handle scripture that's on the surface. It does not have the spiritual mind to receive revelation knowledge that carries you beneath the surface *(Ephesians 1:17; 1 Corinthians 2:14)*. The natural or carnal minded man couldn't handle it because it seems foolish to him, especially religious preachers who have been indoctrinated in their tradition.

> *"And it came to pass, when Jesus had ended these sayings, **THE PEOPLE WERE ASTONISHED AT HIS DOCTRINE: FOR HE TAUGHT THEM AS ONE HAVING AUTHORITY,** and not as the scribes."*
> ***(Matthew 7:28-29)***

There was something different about Jesus' preaching from that of the scribes or the traditionalists of His day. He taught with authority. When I began to teach and preach with authority, the traditionalists began to label me as a heretic. I never had much problem with the common lay people. Many of them would tell me how they would leave their church to get home in time enough to hear my Sunday afternoon broadcast on the radio.

> *"...And the **COMMON PEOPLE** heard him gladly."*
> ***(Mark 12:37b)***

The only lay people who gave me problems were those who were influenced and indoctrinated by their pastors.

> *"And therefore did **THE JEWS PERSECUTE JESUS, AND SOUGHT TO SLAY HIM,** because he had done these things on the Sabbath day. Therefore the **JEWS SOUGHT THE MORE TO KILL HIM,** because he not only had broken the Sabbath, but said also that God was his Father, making himself equal with God."*
> ***(John 5:16,18)***

Once Jesus challenged their traditions, they sought to persecute and kill him. Praise God, my persecutors have yet to try to kill me physically, but they worked to kill me with their tongues. When I became a Bishop in the Full Gospel Baptist Church Fellowship, I received word how I was the topic of one of the minister's alliance sessions. My picture and newsletter was distributed among the pastors to seek a way to counteract Full Gospel teachings.

I lost preacher or pastor friends who could no longer be affiliated with me. Pastors I used to preach for stopped calling me to come and preach. For a while, my brother had distanced himself from me because of who he was in the Baptist denomination. I understood him and somewhat expected it. I'm sure my change had to be somewhat of an embarrassment for him. Here I was, his Baptist brother, now talking in tongues.

I would go to other traditional churches for special occasions and had to listen to pastors throw hints from the pulpit or even call my name out. One preacher in particular wanted to be the one who could say he was the one that got A. R. Williams. I was teaching at a Baptist institute and all of the classes had reunited in the auditorium. This pastor went after me from the beginning. When it was over, I wanted to go somewhere and hide. He was also one of the pastors who I used to preach for that quit calling me. The institute just happened to be at his church, but another pastor invited me. When it was over, a lady who was in the audience came up and apologized for his remarks toward me. Another preacher came up and said, "Well tomorrow night you are on to give the opening address, that'll be your time."

I went home with revenge thoughts on my mind. Finally, the Holy Ghost said, "I want you to walk in love toward him tomorrow night. I want you to honor and esteem him. Do not make **ME** look bad." God was saying to me that I represented Him and His agenda, not my own. I'm preaching for Him, not myself. When Moses got angry at the people, he made the same mistake by "smiting" the rock twice when God told him to speak to the rock. He made God look bad in the eyes of the people and missed the promised land *(Numbers 20:7-12)*.

Man, I began to repent, but immediately peace came when I decided I would not fight back. I knew God had a promised life or an inheritance for me that I could not afford to miss. You will miss it if you get distracted into being offended by men.

The next night, I was first on the program and I must admit flesh still wanted to do something to get even. But the moment I got up, the love of God flooded my heart. I went to the platform and I began to esteem him as if we were the best of friends. I told of what he meant to our city and the great work he had done and how he was one of my favorite pastors.

When it was over and he came to the platform to close the service, you could tell that coals of fire were all over his head.

"Therefore if thine enemy hunger, feed him; if he thirst, give him drink: for in so doing **THOU SHALT HEAP COALS OF FIRE ON HIS HEAD."**
(Romans 12:20)

The previous night he would not call me "Bishop Williams," not that I am into titles, but I knew he didn't want to give me that honor. When I finished, he called me "Bishop" and began to esteem me as I had esteemed him. He had been shown up. The people, and especially preachers, were waiting for me to get back. Even after the services were over and we stood around mingling, several pastors complimented me for showing love and not fighting back.

"Be not overcome of evil, but **OVERCOME EVIL WITH GOOD."**
(Romans 12:21)

If you are going to successfully go through the persecution, you must overcome evil with good and walk in God's divine love because love never fails. Satan will present you many opportunities to be offended *(Luke 17:1)*. If you fail in this area like Moses, you too will miss your promised land.

Whenever you begin walking by the Word of God, Satan

comes immediately to take away the Word that has been sown in your heart *(Mark 4:15)*. God gives five things Satan uses against us to pressure us out of the word: affliction, **PERSECUTION** *(v. 17)*, cares of this world, deceitfulness of riches and the lust of other things *(v. 19)*.

Satan uses persecution to put pressure on you to abandon your commitment to the Word of God. When people are talking against you and ostracizing themselves from you, it's part of Satan's plan to get you to turn around. It's a part of human nature to want to be accepted by our peers and family. That's why it's so hard.

The blessings, however, of God's hundredfold return will come, only through persecution.

*"But he shall receive an **HUNDREDFOLD** now in this time...**WITH PERSECUTIONS**..."*

(Mark 10:30)

Jesus said, "if they have persecuted me, they will also persecute you" *(John 15:20)*. *1 Peter 4:14* says:

*"If ye be reproached for the name of Christ, happy are ye; **FOR THE SPIRIT OF GLORY AND OF GOD RESTETH UPON YOU:** on their part he is evil spoken of, but on your part, he is glorified.*

God says: if you are being reproached because of His name, the spirit and glory of God are resting upon you. Persecution means that for the first time in your Christian walk you have begun to look like your Savior. While I walked as a traditional pastor, nobody talked about me. No one ever persecuted me. I heard somebody say, if no one is talking against or about you negatively, it's a sign you must be walking with the devil.

"Woe unto you, when all men shall speak well of you!.."

(Luke 6:26a)

When you begin to push the agenda of Jesus and His Word, you will get the same results as Jesus got and that was persecution. When I started talking about the Holy Ghost, tongues, healing, and lifting hands to praise God, all hell broke loose. I now understand why. His Spirit was resting upon me. The devil in them has recognized the Jesus in me. **THE GOOD NEWS OF PERSECUTION IS THAT YOU HAVE BEGUN TO LOOK LIKE JESUS.**

"Remember the word that I said unto you, The servant is not greater than his lord. **IF THEY HAVE PERSECUTED ME, THEY WILL ALSO PERSECUTE YOU;** *if they have kept my sayings, they will keep yours also. But all these things will they do unto you for my name's sake, because they know not him that sent me."*

(John 15:20-21)

The reason people persecute is because they don't know God or His Word. People who know God will keep His sayings and accept His truth. Therefore, when you are teaching His truth, if they know God, they will accept your sayings. If they persecute you because of the Word you preach, it is because they have not accepted God or the fullness of His Word. Persecution will come because most people know religion, but they don't know God and His Word.

For strength in persecution, see the following scriptures: *Matthew 5:11,44; Luke 6:22-23; 2 Timothy 3:11.*

10
WALKING BY FAITH

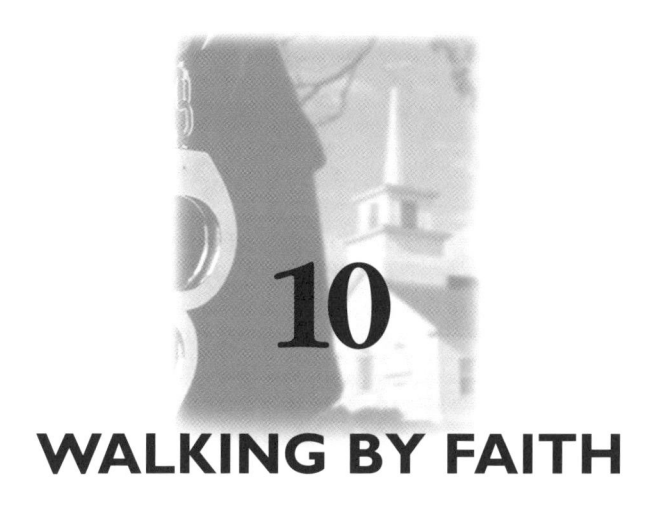

When God began to move on my spirit to leave the church in 1988-89, I did exactly what Bro. Keith Moore's prophecy told us not to do. Rather than pray, I started trying to figure out what God was doing. I started thinking that maybe the Lord is getting ready to send us to a church somewhere in the country that was more conducive to what I had learned at Rhema. Rhema had a ministry placement service to help students from Rhema find churches to pastor. I applied but never found the church that fit us.

After resigning in January of 1989, the deacons asked if I would operate as acting pastor, continue to oversee the church and make decisions while they prepared to find a new pastor. They said they would continue to pay my salary until they found someone. Once again, God was providing for me. When I resigned, my mind was set to get out and make it on my own. Looking back on it, however, I found out that they were trying to hold on to me because they thought that I wasn't sure and would ultimately change my mind and come back.

I must admit there was a part of me that was also glad that I was leaving because the last thing I wanted to do was change what people called "my daddy's church." I knew that what I had learned would not sit well with this traditional Baptist church. My father however, had laid a great foundation and had taught his people well.

MY QUIET WAR WITH MY MOTHER

I was also glad because of the quiet war that went on between my mother, sister and me. My family had been somewhat used to doing what they wanted to in the church. My father gave that power to my mother, and my sister, as I stated earlier, was like her main assistant.

When I began to pastor the church and make demands and decisions contrary to what they were used to, that's when the war began. I began confronting my sister to get in line with my authority. It wasn't easy for her. I was her younger brother. Now all of a sudden her "kid brother" was telling her what to do. Moses had to go through the same thing with his older sister, Miriam. She had nursed Moses as a child *(Exodus 2:4)*. She was the one who led him to safety as a baby in the river and now all of a sudden, he was her leader *(Numbers 12:1-15)*.

When you have been the pastor's kids for so long, you tend to think you have free reign to do as you want, because your father is the pastor. We never saw Dad as "pastor," he was "Daddy." Therefore, we never really learned to respect pastoral authority.

In April of 1984, after I confronted my sister about getting to rehearsal on time and had her pay docked (she was the director of the choir), she gave me her letter of resignation. I knew that she was really not ready to quit. I also knew I could not ask her to come back, because if she knew that I needed her and had to depend on her, I would no longer be the pastor of the church. My mother tried to find ways to use my sister in the church through the "back door" without coming through me. One Sunday, as my mother conducted the congregational hymn, she called my sister up to finish the song. As my sister approached the floor podium, I stood up in the pulpit, extended my hand in the "police stop" position and told her not to come up. That was the day the war started. I probably could have done it another way, but I knew I had to win their respect. I also knew that I had to win the respect of my church. I knew they were watching. If I let my family get by, I would have to let others do it also.

My wife was serving as the church's organist and main musician. Because of my conflict with my sister, a conflict ultimately developed between my mother and my wife. My mother was feeling for my sister.

My mother influenced the church with her very presence. In most denominational churches, where the pastor is not the pastor, there is usually somebody that controls that church other than the pastor; a family or several families; an ex-first lady whose husband served as pastor for many years and has a lot of influence or a deacon and/or trustee. Sometimes, it may be an assistant minister who wants the top position and works underhandedly to undermine the pastor.

My mother had the power to sit on that second row pew in the middle aisle and if she didn't like somebody's singing, speaking, or preaching, almost the whole church wouldn't like it. I would see my wife <u>try</u> to sing and the whole church sat frigid cold on her. My mother had that kind of control.

My mother would sometimes express her feelings to a few people in the church; they would in turn pass it on to others in the church. We started seeing people's attitudes change toward us, especially my wife. We heard comments made such as, "There will never be another first lady like Mrs. J. W."; "Can't nobody take Mrs. J. W.'s place"; "We're not going to let anybody move Mrs. J.W. out of the way." I figured out that Momma had shared that with some of the members, and this was what they were thinking. We saw people openly throw hints in church and sometimes to us one-on-one.

I saw people hurt my wife's feelings many, many times. We got so tired of all the church games. We just wanted to go somewhere and truly worship Jesus. That's why going to Tulsa was like a beautiful, extended vacation. We were ready to leave it all. I remember telling the deacons when I finally resigned in 1989 that the church would not progress until my mother changed. She had too much influence. I inherited a majority of members who were following her and the church values of her generation, and I knew they would not be able to follow me.

My wife's problem was that she always wanted to be accepted in the flow of the church and fit in. When that didn't happen, she was hurt deeply. I felt her hurt and pain and many times she had only me to vent it on. I saw her shed many tears. There were times she wanted to talk to me about what she was going through in the church, and I told her I didn't want to hear it. I was wrong. I was feeling the pressure of being between my wife and my family and it affected me when I was in the pulpit. It almost caused a rift to develop between us. Had it not been for my knowledge of what *Matthew 19:5* said, we could have divorced. Many couples break under family pressure and intervention.

*"And said, For this cause shall **A MAN LEAVE FATHER AND MOTHER**, and shall **CLEAVE TO HIS WIFE**: and they twain shall be one flesh?"*

That scripture and our love for each other endured this great test. There were times my wife could have fought back, and in the natural probably should have, but she wouldn't. She kept walking in love and as a result, today God has raised her up and is using her greatly. She has been a hundredfold recipient with me. I am where I am today, because of her love and obedience to God. When I got ready to leave Memphis and go somewhere we had never been before and all her security was in jeopardy, she said, "Wherever God sends you, I'm with you." Had she challenged my faith and what God was telling me, we quite possibly could have missed our destiny.

I need to also say my family meant no great harm to me. They were only trying to hold on to the one thing that meant the most to them and protect the foundations of what they had believed all their lives as Baptists. To them, it was like I was about to uproot their entire belief system. The church was my mother's life and it was the only life she had. When you have had a certain degree of power, attention, admiration, and affection as a pastor's wife, it is not easy to relinquish that. The enemy allowed my mother to feel threatened by my wife and me. Regardless of the many honor days that I gave her, Momma was just used to being in charge. She probably also did not understand the change that I went through.

THE TRUE TEST OF FAITH BEGINS

I stayed on as pastor for another two months. My mother told me that the people could not go on until they knew I was out of the way. I informed her that the deacons were the ones that asked me to stay. Not wanting the church to be confused, I came back to the church the second Sunday in March 1989 to make the resignation final.

The true test was now on. For the first time in my life, I did not have the church or family to fall back on. For the next seven to eight months I lived by faith and the last of my savings. It was during this time I experienced those little miraculous provisions that I told you about earlier. It was also a time of great wandering, bewilderment, and uncertainty. I searched for the way to take care of my family. I tried a security guard job; I worked a janitorial job for one night and went home half dead. I tried a telemarketing job. You would dial 30-40 telephone numbers and hear the phone hang up in your face 75% of the time. I made about $23 for an eight-hour day. I applied for a job at a Christian TV station, but they were not hiring. I even made attempts to go into business as a videographer, a car detailer, and an automobile consultant. I bought business kits for credit consulting, real estate and upholstery refurbishing. Nothing worked. I even received a prophetic word that God wanted me to use this time to seek Him, because He was preparing me for what was ahead. I just could not do it, because I've always been the breadwinner and I did not like the idea of no longer being able to provide for my family. My wife's job at American Airlines was the only income we had.

After my graduation from Rhema in May of 1989, I applied for a position at Rhema. I felt that because I had pastoral experience and most students didn't, they should have given me a position in that area. It never happened.

Someone told me that you will never get on at Rhema without putting your hand to something and becoming faithful. Since I didn't know what my future would be, I began serving in the ministry. During Camp Meeting in late July of that year, I worked at the radio ministry booth. This was a very humbling experience for me. I had been a pastor and now was being demoted to the radio booth. I even saw pastors from Memphis that I knew, but God was teaching me faithfulness and humility. He showed me that **THE MINISTRY** was more important than my ministry. When you love God and **THE** ministry, you will be willing to serve God anywhere. I even served in the youth ministry at Rhema for a brief time.

Allow me to go back to the security guard job. In the month of October, I had been employed by a security guard service. I went in that Friday night about 10:30 p.m. with my hard hat and blue shirt. I was home by 1:30 a.m. after they told me about the skunks. My friend, who helped me to get the job, told me that they will give you the worst jobs unless you speak up and ask for a building to work in. I called the supervisor on Saturday morning to tell him that I wanted a building to guard and that I could not handle the job they gave me. We were to meet on Monday morning to receive my new assignment. God intervened however, that same Saturday morning.

11

GOD'S PHONE CALL FOR ME TO RETURN

A friend of mine, who I had met the previous year and had not seen for a year, called me from Pennsylvania at the right time. My wife had gone to work and I was "Mr. Mom" keeping the house and the kids. I was washing the dishes when I answered the telephone. This gentleman was a pastor and knew from the previous year that I was considering leaving the church. We had not talked since, and he never knew that I had resigned. He said that I came up in his prayer that morning. He asked, "Alton, is God dealing with you about that church and going back to it?" I told him all that had happened to me and what was happening in the church. They elected a pastor in July after I resigned. Just as quick as he was elected, he was ousted. He came in without a mandate from the congregation. The election really represented the desire of those in the church to have a candidate elected that would give them favor and power.

The church had just voted him out the week I received this call from my friend. He said, "Alton it seems like nothing is going right for them or you. Go back and let the people know you are there if they want you. If they reject you, then you will know it's a closed door. Lane Avenue will be a closed chapter in your life. Otherwise, it will always be in your mind that you left them, not that they got rid of you." He said, "Go back and see what the Lord does. That could be the reason things have not gone well for either of you. That may be your place after all."

MY FIRST ASSIGNMENT AS AN APOSTLE AND I DIDN'T KNOW IT

The word *"apostle"* means "to be sent" or "a sent one." God was sending me back home, I could tell. I knew the Lord was speaking because this guy had no way of knowing what was going on in my life at that time. This was now October of 1989. By this time the person who had been voted in to succeed me as pastor in July had now been voted out. He did not have a mandate by the congregation to begin with. He was, however, the preacher that my mother wanted, because she had hopes of ruling the church through him.

THE CHURCH GOES TO COURT

It was discovered that the minister had a previous police record and some members felt that he was spending too much of the church's money. There was a little truth about the spending, although some of it was blown out of proportion. The real problem was that there were two main groups that wanted power in the church. No one cared about the will of God. This goes on in most independent autonomous denominational congregations, such as Baptist churches. The group who did not get their person in as pastor was trying to find a way to get this man out of office. The situation came to a head on a Sunday morning and the church divided. One group brought newspapers and read them while the minister preached that Sunday. The other group dressed in black and staged a walk out. The pastor was ultimately put out of the church. His supporters, which included my family members and some of the top leading members of our church, left with him. This group ultimately got an attorney, and the case went to court. The church and its officials were sued by the opposing side. Many black Baptist churches end disputes like this in the world's court system. The reason is tradition makes the Word of God of none effect. We are so bound to our traditions until we never see the Word of God. His Word never makes an impact on our lives. Most people in the church don't know any better because they have not been taught the Word of God. Churches learn their denomination's doctrines and creeds through the Sunday School Quarterly. Most churches don't even know what the Bible says about going to court.

*"**DARE ANY OF YOU,** having a matter against another, **GO TO LAW** before the unjust, and not before the saints? Do ye not know that the saints shall judge the world? And if the world shall be judged by you, are ye unworthy to judge the smallest matters? Know ye not that we shall judge angels? How much more things that pertain to this life? If then ye have judgments of things pertaining to this life, set them to judge who are least esteemed in the church. I speak to your shame. Is it so, that there is not a wise man among you? No, not one that shall be able to judge between his brethren? But brother goeth to law with brother, and that before the unbelievers. Now therefore there is utterly a fault among you, because ye go to law one with another. **WHY DO YE NOT RATHER TAKE WRONG? WHY DO YE NOT RATHER SUFFER YOURSELVES TO BE DEFRAUDED?"***

(1 Corinthians 6:1-7)

Verse 7 is the **REASON** why churches end up in court cases. Because the Word of God has not penetrated the hearts of people, they still have their carnal, fleshly, selfish ways *(1 Corinthians 3:1-4)*. There is strife, selfish ambition, jealousy, bitterness, confusion and revenge that takes place in these situations *(James 3:14-16)*.

In *verse 7* Paul told the carnal Corinthian church "**WHY DO YE NOT RATHER TAKE WRONG?** Why do ye not rather suffer yourselves to be defrauded?" Nobody is willing to suffer loss for the sake of God's Kingdom. Rather than move on if you can't agree and trust the Lord to order your steps, we'd rather kick, argue, scratch, fight and go to court and make God's house look bad, which is what happens when we go to court.

The pastor that was voted out sued the head of the deacon and trustee board. This was done so they could say they were not suing the church, but in actuality, it was still the church being sued because the court placed an injunction on all of the church's finances. The money was frozen and could not be used. Therefore, it was the church being sued. The two church officials did not have their finances frozen. Also Paul didn't necessarily mention the church being sued. He spoke about brother taking brother to court *(verse 6)*.

The judge sent the church back to have another election. With the Pastor and his followers outside of the church and not willing to come back, of course, he lost overwhelmingly and unanimously.

THE DAY I CAME BACK

It was in this kind of atmosphere that I returned. When I called the deacon board chairman that Sunday morning, I asked him if I could come by and speak to the people. I told him I had heard that the morale of the people was very low due to the split. He eagerly accepted my request.

I remember that morning as if it were yesterday. As I walked in, some people were glad to see me and responded in applause, others stood or sat in shock while others were totally upset. Some were not sure what my motives were. Some people I heard thought that my family was sending me back to obtain control of the church. When I went to the podium, I couldn't do anything but cry. I cried for about a good five minutes while many of them cried with me. I apologized to them if I caused them any grief over my leaving. After sharing with them for a few moments, I told them what was happening to me, and that if they still wanted me, I was willing to come back. If they didn't, I would move on. I proposed to them that since the church was still in court, I would serve as acting pastor until an election was official.

I was not willing to go through an election against other candidates. I told them that they had two choices: vote for me as pastor or vote to open the floor for other candidates and have an election. If they voted for an election, that would say to me that they didn't want me. I told them if they didn't elect me, I would help them in any way I could to give them the leadership they needed to get another pastor. The church ultimately voted for me, through much opposition from the group who wanted the power.

We noticed that every Sunday the pastor who was voted out would show up with a few of his followers. He would make the attempt to come preach. The deacons would tell him "No" and they would turn around and leave. This started a few Sundays before I came back. The second Sunday, I was there when it happened again. I remember walking to the back of the church during worship service. I was about to preach when the ex-pastor and his followers showed up. I stood at the glass church doors in the back as the chairman of the deacon board told him he could not preach. As I stood there, I looked to the right at his followers. People that I had pastored for years were now estranged from the church and me. Also there in that line was my oldest sister who I loved, now on the opposite side of the fence from me.

I saw the hurt and anger in her eyes, but what she did not know, was that I was crying on the inside too. For the first time in my life, my family was my foe *(Matthew 10:36)*. I had a first hand experience of that sword Jesus talked about that would divide a family *(Matthew 10:34)*. It was the toughest time of my life. I still could not understand why they were showing up every Sunday at worship time. What were they trying to accomplish by doing that? I came over to the church one night and I began to seek the Lord.

I prayed and asked the Lord to show me what was going on. He led me to the church's by-laws that I had instituted before I left. I found a clause that stated that if the pastor was turned off from the church, he would receive six-months of whatever his salary was at the time of his dismissal. If they did not pay it he would keep getting his salary each week until the six-month severance pay was paid. That means each week he showed up to preach and was denied access to the pulpit, because the church had not paid the severance he was making $700 a week. **BINGO!** I found it. Our church board did not see this. I had to come back and reveal to them that if the church did not pay the severance and the salary that had added up each week since they fired him – each week he showed up, it was another $700. Of course, the ex-pastor was aware that the church had approximately $160,000 in the bank and could pay it. He and his attorney knew what they were doing.

I had this clause placed in the by-laws for protection for my family and me. I had given up my high school teaching career after four years in order to give myself to full-time pastoring. Knowing how people sometimes change, I could be out without anything for my family and I needed some security. That six-month severance would give me time to hopefully find another job. The mistake that the deacons and trustees made was they did not take my advice before I officially resigned. I told them to get the by-laws changed before they elected a new pastor. That clause was placed in there for me for the sacrifice I made for my teaching career. They never did it.

We had a church meeting one night, and I told them that if they did not pay this money, it was going to cost the church. Many of the members were hostile over the split already. They felt that he didn't deserve six months of salary, which could have been at least $18,000. He had only been there less than two months. They felt he had spent money he should not have spent for himself and the church. He had hired people and put them on the payroll giving them large salaries they didn't deserve. So the people were crushed when they found out they had to give him that much money.

I knew that the judge however, was going to make the church honor those by-laws and the longer they waited to pay that severance, the more they would have to pay in the end.

*"And if any man will sue thee at the law, and take away thy coat, **LET HIM HAVE THY CLOAK ALSO."***

(Matthew 5:40)

QUALIFYING A PASTOR

That's why it is so important that churches learn how to qualify a pastor. The traditional church only used preaching ability to gauge whether or not he would make a good pastor. In many black Baptist churches, whoever could hoop, holler, and move the church emotionally the best, would win the election. Character was usually never an issue. Churches would argue, fight, and get in strife over a pastoral election. Yet, nobody would ever think to pray and seek God. Every "clique" had their candidate. Some were trying to get their relatives, friend, or children in as pastor.

The Word of God emphasizes character, home life, and integrity more than a minister's talents, gifts, and preaching abilities. *1 Timothy 3:1-5* gives the qualifications of a pastor or church leader. It talks about being married, having the right behavior, being more apt to teach than preach, abstaining from drugs or alcohol, not greedy for money, not a fighter, ruling his house and children well; their home life had to be right. If churches would use this as a gauge, before electing a pastor, it would save a lot of problems in the future. The ex-pastor hardly had any of these qualities. He came in one Sunday, did a "hoop and holler" message, and he won the election by a small majority. He never had a mandate from the congregation.

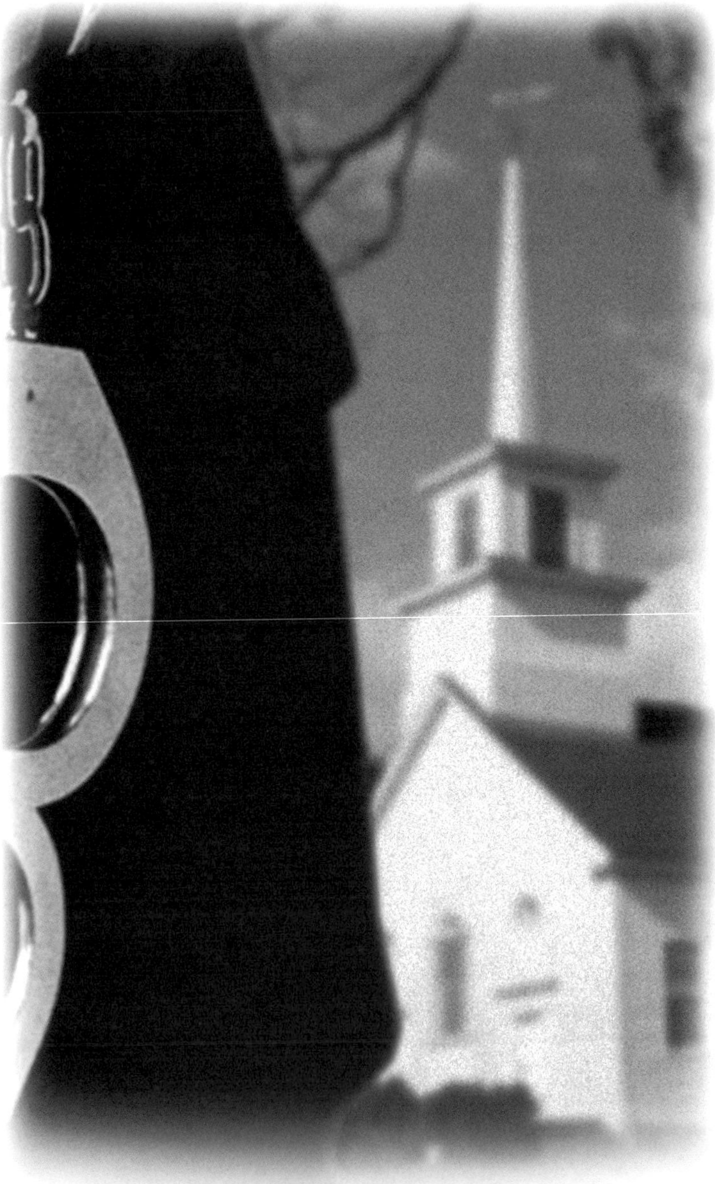

12

THE BEGINNING OF THE CHURCH'S TRANSFORMATION

SATAN'S LAST STAND

Those in the church who wanted the power and did not want me to come back began to use the court case as a means of keeping me from being elected as permanent pastor for the second time. With having to travel back and forth on the weekends, if the case is held out, maybe I would get tired and would quit coming. I was determined, however, to see the church through until we were out of court. I felt I owed it to the church, because they were somewhat in this situation because of my leaving.

I even saw where the lawyers representing both sides were probably working together to drag the process out. It meant more money for the lawyers. Satan was working to destroy this church and keep it from ultimately reaching its purpose and destiny. This was a very crucial time. The Lord's finances for His church was at stake. This church had a date with destiny.

The attorney representing our church was hired by those who were desiring the power. I was not getting any cooperation from the attorney at all. He was not trying to get the church out of its injunction. I knew his strings were being pulled by those who hired him. I had to apply some pressure. I began to meet with the church to openly expose what was going on. The church had given me the power to pay the former pastor his severance pay. The check was to be prepared, but instead, it was not carried to the attorney's office. The money was used to buy an expensive copy machine. All of this was designed to stall and hinder me from being elected because the opposition in the church led the church to believe that there could be no election until the case was settled. That could have taken months.

I called a meeting with the church to reveal what had happened and that the money had not been paid. Each week I would keep the church informed so that they could see what was happening, and they would ultimately find where the problem was. That evening I saw the Spirit of God move in such a mighty way. Those who were wanting control turned on each other right in the meeting. They began pointing fingers and blaming each other for what had taken place. They wilted under the pressure.

*"...And **THE LORD SET EVERY MAN'S SWORD AGAINST HIS FELLOW**, even throughout all the host: and the host fled..."*
(Joshua 7:22)

(See also *1 Samuel 14:20; 2 Chronicles 20:23*)

When you are doing the will of God, He will cause your enemies to turn on each other. He will allow you to see your desire come upon your enemies. When a man's ways please the Lord, He will make even his enemies to be at peace with him. He will cause the enemies that rise up against you to be smitten or defeated before your face. They will come out against you one way and flee before you seven ways *(Psalm 92:11; Proverbs 16:7; Deuteronomy 28:7).*

From that point, on I knew I was in control. After speaking to another attorney, I was told that the court case had nothing to do with the church having the right to vote for its own pastor. I shared this with the church. I had asked that we move on with our intent to elect a pastor. I would not allow the church to put me in an election. They had to vote on either me or open the house for other candidates and have an election. The only unresolved issue was the by-laws. The church wanted to be sure that in the event I left again, the same thing would not happen to them. I could definitely understand that. The church chose to go on and elect, because I needed to know what I was going to do with my life. I was elected by a unanimous decision with the stipulation that the by-laws be amended and approved by the congregation. After electing me, we had two weeks before the meeting to approve the by-laws.

I won for two reasons as it relates to how the people were viewing it. The people had been hurt by the previous election and was afraid to go through that process again and trust another stranger. Secondly, many of them thought my coming back would make things as they once were and my family would be back and things would be normal again. They had no idea what was about to happen. God had other plans. Had they known the church was about to change and that God was about to send in a harvest of people, they probably would not have voted me in. Traditional churches love keeping the aquarium of their special fish. They never want to catch new fish. Why? Because they will lose control.

Boy, I remember that By-Laws meeting like it was yesterday. I did everything to bring order to the process, making sure everything was fair. One of the old members from years back, who I had not seen since I first became pastor in 1981, got up and totally disrespected my authority. He challenged my leadership, the by-laws, and everything. The meeting was totally disrupted. I did not try to argue with him. But I remembered that he was one of my father's old enemies. The Holy Spirit spoke to me and told me not to fight or argue back, but to confront him with love. I remember saying:

> '**Bro. _____, you were one of my
> father's old enemies and now I sense you
> have a problem with me. I don't want you
> to be that way with me. We are commanded
> by the Lord to love one another. I want
> you to come here and let me hug you and let's
> put this behind us.**'

We embraced, I cried, the church cried, clapped and rejoiced.

I also knew that even though I was voted in unanimously, those who were opposed did not want to be seen voting contrary to the majority. They knew they had one more chance and that was to find a problem in the by-laws.

GOT TO CHANGE THE BY-LAWS

I took the by-laws and amended them and made concessions based upon their concerns. I even added a statement that no matter what, I would never carry the church to court.

Before the church began to vote on the new amendments, I had heard earlier that day that the opposition had met to organize on how they would stall or sabotage the process. Various ones had been selected to question this, someone else was selected to question that.

Before I passed the newly amended by-laws out for a vote, I made a request to the entire congregation. I said, "I am aware that there are some here who have met with intentions of stalling this process. I pray tonight that you do not hinder the work of God. If you have a legitimate question, you have the right to ask, but please do not hold up the process just because I may not be your favorite candidate." The by-laws passed unanimously.

NO LONGER PASTORING FOR FAMILY

I was pastor for the second time. This time it meant something to me. The first election I felt that I was doing it for family and to make the members happy that there was a "Williams" in office. This time, all the family apron strings were broken. Family had nothing to do with me being elected this time. Because of my mother and sister's departure from the church and statements my mother had made about not ever coming back to the church, the atmosphere was not favorable for a "Williams" to be elected.

My election this time finally signified to me that God had called me to this church. I was sure now. I had come through a great crisis with nobody's help but God. Now with the family strings broken, I could be God's man. I finally felt as though the church was my assignment.

While leaving church the Sunday night after the by-laws were approved, the Spirit of God gave me a simple confirmation that this was where I was supposed to be. Through two years away in school, my resignation, the church's election and ultimate split, the hiring and firing of another pastor, the court case, the inner church conflict, my re-election and the by-laws approval, I looked up at the church's neon lighted sign and my name was still there. The people had never taken it down. It should have come down when my resignation was final. It stayed there from March 1989 - February 1990.

REBUILDING THE WALLS

I finally moved back home in February 1990, and I was down to nothing. I know what it feels like to lose it all for the sake of the Gospel. The church's finances still had an injunction against it. The other group that split from the church never came back except for a few. The morale of the church was low. All I knew to do was to teach the Word, teach the principles I had learned. Suddenly, the church began to grow. There are times the Lord has to subtract from you so that He can begin to add or multiply. The contingency of people that left with the ex-pastor probably would have been the group that resisted the change the most. Sometimes, the Lord has to separate the wheat from the tare. Sometimes, things have to die before they can be resurrected *(Matthew 13:24-20; John 12:24)*.

Part of the work I needed to have done in order to reorganize the church had been done in the split itself. It totally tore down the old system. All I had to do was rebuild and restructure. Most of the members who were still there were very receptive to whatever I brought back to them, because the walls were broken down and had to be rebuilt. This made a way for the Holy Ghost.

LAYING A HOLY GHOST FOUNDATION

I spent the next few months teaching the church on the subject of the Baptism with the Holy Ghost. I taught on it for three months before I ever extended an invitation to receive. Finally, on the Sunday I gave the invitation to be filled with the Holy Ghost, I saw about one half of the congregation receive with the evidence of speaking with other tongues. I had a local pastor friend, Pastor Leo Holt, to come with a few of his trained members to help minister to the people. In later months, Pastor Leroy Bailey and members of his congregation would come in and conduct Holy Ghost meetings and workshops.

THE END OF THE COURT INJUNCTION

In June of that year, after putting much pressure on the attorney representing our church, we were finally free from the court's injunction. Our finances were no longer frozen. The only way I could back the lawyer up was to call other well-known attorneys and judges in the area to let them know what was going on and ask how could we alleviate the problem. Although they did not give me any direct help, it was evident they called him to tell him of my inquiry. He was being embarrassed and therefore had to finalize the case. He even told me that he knew he was being used by those in the church to stall the process of the church. This particular attorney had a reputation for hating preachers. He had prosecuted a well-known Memphis pastor in a church conflict several years before our case. **THANK GOD WE WERE FREE!**

GOD WILL BRING YOU THROUGH

When you set out to be a **TRADITION BUSTER**, you will pay a heavy price. When you work to fight the status quo system, Satan will react to you. His whole desire is to keep the people of God blind. However, the transition from tradition to truth can happen. The Kingdom of God will back you up when you are doing it for the sake of the

Gospel. Once you make the decision to follow God and His Word, no matter what, He will bring you through.

You will be persecuted, ostracized, misunderstood and sometimes even hated, but remember God's Word from *Luke 6:22-23*:

> *"**BLESSED** are ye **WHEN MEN SHALL HATE YOU,** and when they shall **SEPARATE YOU FROM THEIR COMPANY,** and shall **REPROACH YOU,** and **CAST OUT YOUR NAME AS EVIL,** for the Son of Man's sake. **REJOICE YE IN THAT DAY,** and leap for joy: for, behold, **YOUR REWARD IS GREAT IN HEAVEN:** for in the like manner did their fathers unto the prophets"*

If you are being persecuted, start leaping! If you are being talked about, start jumping! If you are being separated and ostracized, jump, because your reward is great in Heaven.

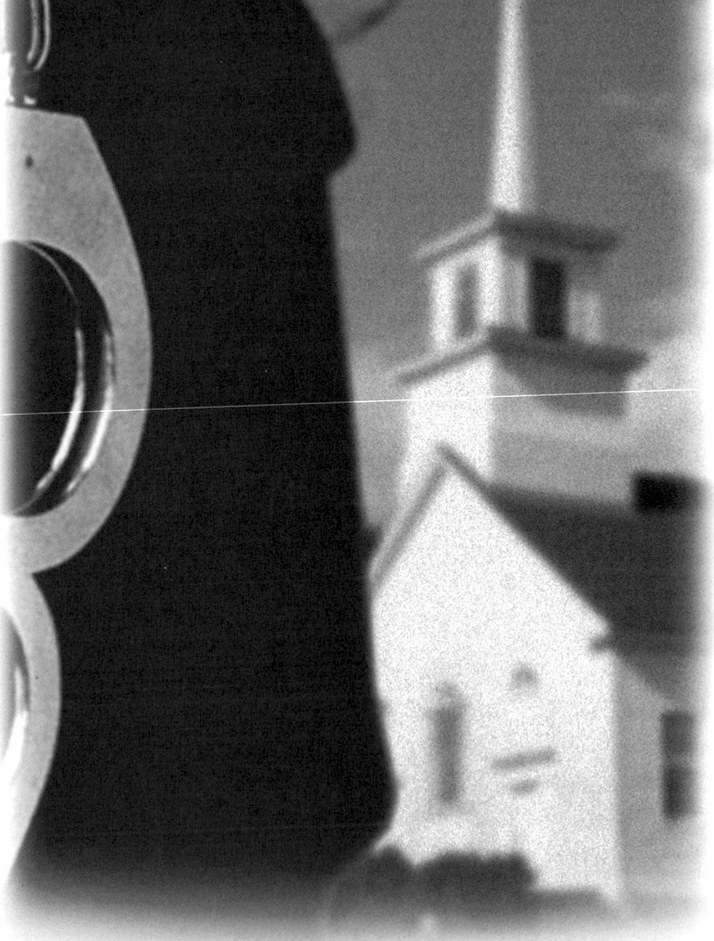

13

THE HUNDREDFOLD MANIFESTATION

Begin rejoicing because Heaven has some things reserved for you not only in Heaven, but now in this time *(Mark 10:30)*. God has blessed my ministry and made it to be a very fruitful one. We have grown from 400-500 members from the time I came back in 1990 to over 4,000 members at the time of this writing.

In October 1995, we made our first growth move. After 51 years of ministry in the North Memphis area, we moved from a 400 capacity seat auditorium to a 900-seat sanctuary in South Memphis. We went in with two services that filled to capacity very quickly. The building was paid for in two years.

THE NAME CHANGE

While in this building in 1997, God changed the name of our ministry from Lane Avenue Full Gospel Baptist Church to World Overcomers Outreach Ministries Church, a non-denominational ministry. The aforementioned name reflected my appointment as a Bishop and one of the founding fathers of the Full Gospel Baptist Church Fellowship. The name change took us to another level of growth. Many people wanted to come to the church but had a problem with the denominational affiliation. They heard the Word inside, but saw another name outside. One lady gave me a prophecy and said that she saw the church congregation sitting in a matchbox with a lid over it. When the name change was announced, she said the lid was removed in the Spirit and now the church was open to God. The lid (denominations) represented man's restrictions on God's house. Without the lid, God could now pour in all of His revelation and blessings from Heaven.

There were several Baptist pastors and church members in the city of Memphis that felt I had something against the Baptist church when I changed the name. What the Baptist church preached as basic doctrine was not wrong. It was very solid in its doctrine on salvation. The teachings would vary from pulpit to pulpit. Some pastors seemed to teach that no matter what you did, it was alright with God, yet on paper the Baptist doctrine was not wrong; it was just lacking of all the many other great and wonderful things that God wants to do for His people.

Although I did not see it at the time, God later showed me His purpose for the name change. His plan for our church was to appeal to more than one segment of the Body of Christ. With "Baptist" on the door, the only people that would come would be people who were looking for a Baptist ministry. Without the label of any one denomination, our church would become like a melting pot of believers from all segments of the Body of Christ. We presently have members from the Baptist, Methodist, Church Of God In Christ, Catholic, Disciples of Christ, Apostolic, Nazarene, Presbyterian, Pentecostal Holiness and others. Let me add that a name change may not be God's plan for everyone. God's plan and purpose for our ministry however, required a name change.

He chose a name that did not reflect any one denomination, but one that reflected who we were as children of God. God says that **BELIEVERS ARE OVERCOMERS** of the world. The name, then, applies to all who believe. God had called us this before we ever chose the name.

*"For whatsoever is born of God overcometh the world: and this is the victory that overcometh the world, even our faith. Who is he that **OVERCOMETH THE WORLD, but HE THAT BELIEVETH** that Jesus is the Son of God?"*

(1 John 5:4-5)

Therefore, according to God's Word if you are a believer, regardless to your denomination, you are a world overcomer whether you like it or not. All believers from all denominations are called overcomers of this world. So why should it be a problem when we decided to call ourselves what God Himself had already called His church?

If people have had bad experiences at a particular denominational church, that's what they will always remember about that denomination. If someone was stealing money; if it was too strict and condemning; if the pastor ran off with another woman, that's what they will always remember. With no denominational tag, we could not be labeled.

With the denominational label removed, people came from everywhere. It worked because it was the plan of God for our church. God has gathered an army to be equipped to go and gather the harvest. God also chose a name that would help my people to always be reminded of who they are in Him. No matter what trial, tribulation, problem or circumstance they were in, it would ring in their ears that they could overcome. Some people have thought that we were saying we were perfect or better than anyone else and that we would never go through anything. However, the word *"overcome"* itself means you have gone through something or otherwise why is there the need to overcome?

Over the years, I have had members to tell me how they were in various trials and the name of the church would pop up in their minds and give them hope and faith: "**YOU ARE A WORLD OVERCOMER.**" It also reflects the great world vision God has for our church. Apostolic vision affects the world for Jesus through missions, prayer and finances. Our desire is to affect the nations of the world by sending missionaries from our church or through prayer. Finally, it is also an end-time prophetic church name. Before the rapture, God told the church world that He would be coming back for an overcoming people.

*"**HE THAT OVERCOMETH,** the same shall be clothed in white raiment; and I will not blot out his name out of the book of life, but I will confess his name before my Father, and before his angels. **HIM** that overcometh will I make a pillar in the temple of my God, and he shall go no more out: and I will write upon him the name of my God, and the name of the city of my God, which is new Jerusalem, which cometh down out of heaven from my God: and I will write upon him my new name. **TO HIM THAT OVERCOMETH** will I grant to sit with me in my throne, even as I also overcame, and am set down with my Father in his throne."*

(Revelation 3:5,12,21)

I thank God for our new identity in Him. No, we have not left the Baptist. God has placed us in the position to make a broader appeal to all segments of the body. He has sent us a remnant of people from all denominations. That's when you know you are crumbling the walls of tradition.

Before leaving the South church on Holmes Road, we were holding three services in that building. We had gotten to the point where people were coming to the main 10:00 a.m. service and could not get in. We were losing potential members. We began to consider building. The church had purchased 12 acres of land a few years earlier in the north part of the city. However, I never sensed the anointing to build and secondly, it would probably take a year and a half to two years to start design and complete a building program. We needed space immediately.

In 1999, we purchased the former First Assembly of God building, a 1700 seat auditorium on Highland Street near the Mid-town part of the city. Once again, we out-grew the facility and moved within a year and a half to our present location in the East part of the city; the former Central Church, a 3700 seat capacity auditorium with offices, day care center, Christian academy, state-of-the-art Family Life Center; a total of 52 acres. Now I understand why God would not allow me to build. He had something better waiting for me. **GOD IS GOOD AND TO HIM BE ALL GLORY AND HONOR.**

RESTORATION OF FAMILY

My Mother

I have seen my family relationships restored. My mother passed in 1994. Even though our church relationship was never a good one, she continued through it all to treat me as a son. Yet, a small cloud was always over our heads when it came to the church. The church was her life, and it was the only life she had.

Jesus loved his mother. His problem came when she tried to intervene in God's plans and purposes. He had to rebuke her at a wedding in Cana:

> *"And the third day there was a marriage in Cana of Galilee; and the mother of Jesus was there: And both Jesus was called, and his disciples, to the marriage. And when they wanted wine, the mother of Jesus saith unto him, they have no wine. Jesus saith unto her,* **'WOMAN, WHAT HAVE I TO DO WITH THEE?** *mine hour is not yet come."*
>
> *(John 2:1-4)*

Mary's humble response probably saved her biblical legacy. Mary still saw him as her son. For a moment she missed the call on His life and felt that because she was His mother, she had a right to tell him what to do.

"*His mother saith unto the servants,*
WHATSOEVER HE SAITH UNTO YOU, DO IT."

(John 2:5)

It is sometimes very difficult for a mother, who has reared a child, to all of a sudden come under that child when he is placed in a position of authority over her.

Had my mother, with the influence she had in the church, been able to say those words in the midst of our struggle in church, things would have never ended the way they did. As stated earlier, my mother left in the split before I came back in 1989.

Whenever a church endures strife and confusion, bitterness can become a by-product of that. Of course, things were said that hurt my mother. For the first time in 45 years, my mother had no one in that pulpit to protect her. My father had pastored for 38 years and I had been there the last seven. Once I was gone, once the authority was out of the pulpit, "somebody let the dogs out." People made statements like, "The Williams' day was over and it's time for Mrs. J. W. to sit down." You will find that many church people don't necessarily love you as much as they love the authority, power and influence you have. Once that is gone, their true colors will usually come out.

My mother left and never came back. Pride will sometimes carry you too far and make you stay too long. She made statements out of her hurt that probably made it difficult for her to return. She left with the ex-pastor along with approximately 40-50 other members of the church. They made an attempt to organize and purchase another church, but it did not work. At some point, the ex-pastor began to resist her influence. Having left Lane Avenue, they now had no need for each other any more. The ex-pastor needed her influence to get the church. My mother needed somebody she felt would protect her and not cast her to the side as many churches do to their former first ladies. When that need was gone, they no longer had a need for each other. She left the ex-pastor after only a few months and joined with another congregation.

Before she passed, however, we made our peace with one another as it pertained to the church. That year (1994), the church was celebrating its 50th year anniversary. She was sick at the time, but I told her that I wanted her to at least come back for the church anniversary. She consented immediately – if she felt OK. She died the day before the church anniversary program. Her approval to come said to me she had released what had happened in the past. I believe Momma was really just waiting to be asked. Even though she left the church bitter and made statements about never coming back, I knew there was no way she could not have some type of service at the church she worked, and helped my father to organize. I insisted on a service being at the church knowing that she was willing to come back before she passed. She ended up having two funeral services, one at Lane Avenue on that Friday night and the other one at the church where she was a member, Greater Mt. Moriah Missionary Baptist Church on Wellington Street in Memphis. I thank Pastor J. L. Payne, and his church family for providing my mother with a comfortable place of worship during her last years.

She deserved the service at Lane Avenue, because my mother was the catalyst that raised the money to build that church. She was the church musician, Sunday school and Educational Director, and she organized church programs. She had the awesome ability to motivate people to work and serve in the church.

Looking back on it, it was all in the plan of God. If I had taken my authority as pastor and come down on my mother, I would have lost the respect of my members. At that time, my mother could do no wrong. My sister's greatest desire was to help my mother in whatever way she could in order to protect her. That was the extent of her involvement. Most of the church didn't even see what was going on. They would have said things like, "He mistreated his mother." The only way I would be able to effectively pastor the church was if my mother changed or left. God had to do it for me. He caused me to resign, which ultimately took away her power, caused her to leave on her own, and then brought me back without the family control. I now fully understood God's purpose for my resignation. You have to trust God even when it looks foolish *(1 Corinthians 1:27)*.

Had my mother however, said to the church like Mary, *"WHATSOEVER HE SAITH UNTO YOU, DO IT,"* things would have been totally different. Yet, I thank God for His grace and restoring power before she died.

My Sister

My sister left with my mother and joined Greater Mt. Moriah. After joining one other church and experiencing a time of restlessness, I knew she was hurting, confused, grieving and didn't know which way to go. I reached out to her and began ministering to her on the telephone. I invited her to a service we were having one night. She came and received the Holy Ghost. She is now a member of our church serving in the New Members Orientation Ministry and the choir. She allowed God to work in her heart, and her life has never been the same. She stepped out of tradition and allowed the Word of God to have effect in her life. I am so proud of her. She's told me many times, "I just didn't know." Believe me, I understood her. My family didn't know what I was doing. They thought I was going crazy. To be honest with you, I didn't understand me either, but praise God it's all in the past, and I thank Him for a hundredfold restoration with my sister.

My Brother

My brother and I were restored in May of 1993. After about three silent years of us not communicating much, he called me one Tuesday morning. As I said earlier, my change from Baptist tradition had to be somewhat tough for him especially when it came to his ministerial peers in

Memphis. My brother was probably at this time the most well-known black Baptist preacher in the country, and is to this day.

One night while talking to him on the telephone however, long after all of the conflict was over, he acknowledged to me that it was wrong for them to try to stop me from being who I wanted to be. Over the years, we have become very close. One of the greatest honors I've had was to preach at his church in recent years. Although our belief systems are different on some issues, we do respect each other's ministry.

God had to allow a rift in order that I pursue His direction for my life. My brother had such a great influence on my ministry, and in many respects, my life. When he talked, you listened. To this day, I seek his wisdom on many things. I don't believe that any other black Baptist preacher in the country has had the impact and influence on a whole generation of preachers as my brother. Once again, I thank God for a hundredfold restoration.

My Father's Legacy

Finally, for years I had to struggle with my father's legacy. I stepped in some big shoes when I followed him as pastor in 1981. I loved, honored, and respected him and his legacy. However, I had great pressures on me to continue what he started. People always compared us and would not let me be me. Yet, I knew God had another plan for my life and ministry. God would not call me to lead in the same manner by which my father lead the church. Moses lead the children of Israel with a rod. God primarily did everything for them through Moses and that rod, but Joshua was called to lead in a different manner. He lead the people by a sword. By this time the people knew their God and were instructed to fight for themselves with the help of God.

My members could not go forward with my leadership, because they were always looking back to the past. The spirit of tradition always focuses on the past. They are heritage-driven. They are more concerned with what was done in the past; "Let's get back to our roots;" "Let's pray that God makes us what we used to be." They always want to memorialize their founders.

In the early days, my church wanted to always honor my father's memory. I used to have to hear the church's radio broadcast narrator say every week as she closed her announcement: "the late Rev. Jasper W. William, Sr., founder and builder. Rev. A. R. Williams, Pastor." Dad had died, but was always recognized and mentioned first. In the beginning it did not bother me. We were all still grieving somewhat after his death. As time went by, however, it never stopped. One pastor told me that after listening to the radio broadcast one Sunday that he heard my daddy's name more than he did Jesus. That got to me. I also began to realize that my father's memory was being used to send me quiet messages: "As long as you keep what he instituted, you will be alright with us." Sometimes when people wanted to quietly fight me, the message was, "Your daddy is still our leader, not you."

*"For to him that is joined to all the living there is hope: **FOR A LIVING DOG IS BETTER THAN A DEAD LION.**"*

(Ecclesiastes 9:4)

My daddy was like the great lion in comparison to my ministry. I was more like the dog. God says, "I don't care how great the lion was in all of his fierce strength and courage; if it is dead, a dog that is living is greater." In other words, you have no hope with someone that is dead.

THE SIN OF EXALTING AND MEMORIALIZING MAN

Tradition wants to always memorialize its past leaders. Some denominations have named their buildings after the man, etched his image in the stained glass windows of the buildings, and have buried his body in or near the church.

God had to rebuke Peter about this very thing in *Matthew 17*, while on the Mountain of Transfiguration.

*"And after six days Jesus taketh Peter, James, and John his brother, and bringeth them up into an high mountain apart, And was transfigured before them: and his face did shine as the sun, and his raiment was white as the light. And, behold, there appeared unto them Moses and Elias talking with him. Then answered Peter, and said unto Jesus, Lord, it is good for us to be here: if thou wilt, **LET US MAKE HERE THREE TABERNACLES; ONE FOR THEE, AND ONE FOR MOSES, AND ONE FOR ELIAS.** While he yet spake, behold, a bright cloud overshadowed them: and behold a voice out of the cloud, which said, This is my beloved Son, in whom I am well pleased, hear ye him."*

(Matthew 17:1-5)

Peter wanted to erect a building to honor and memorialize previous great men such as Moses and Elijah. God spoke and told them to hear only Jesus. After falling on their faces for a while, the disciples were afraid.

"And when they had lifted up their eyes,
THEY SAW NO MAN, SAVE JESUS ONLY."

(Matthew 17:8)

God caused Moses and Elijah to disappear. When the disciples looked up, only Jesus was left standing. The message was only Jesus should be exalted, reverenced, honored, and followed, not men of the past who have died, gone home and whose assignments are finished. Now you know if Moses and Elijah did not deserve to have a building named for them, who else qualifies? After all, who else can say they were used by God to open up a sea or caused fire to rain down from heaven? No man to this day knows where Moses' body is buried. Only God knows where his grave is located. Why? So that people would not make a shrine out of it to be worshipped. Considering the great things God did through Moses, people would come from near and far to worship that tomb and touch it, instead of seeking after God.

*"So Moses the servant of the Lord died there in the land of Moab, according to the word of the Lord. And he buried him in a valley in the land of Moab, over against Bethpeor: **BUT NO MAN KNOWETH OF HIS SEPULCHER UNTO THIS DAY.**"*

(Deuteronomy 34:5-6)

I must admit that as time went on I began to inwardly resent my father's memory and I knew if I said anything to try to change it, people would say, "He's jealous or threatened by his father's memory." So I let it go on and on. I began to feel like a pawn; that I was only there to continue my father's work and keep family happy. I had vision from God, but it was like nobody wanted to move forward. I later realized that it was never my father's memory or legacy that I resented; instead it was the people using it against me. It came from people who never wanted to see me succeed to begin with. Some were envious; some just did not want to follow my leadership. It was amazing to me to see people who were against my father when he lived all of a sudden fall in love with him in death. People threw his memory at me as psychological warfare against me.

Also to some, my success and God's favor on my ministry meant that God was blessing and honoring what I was doing and teaching. If what I'm doing is right, and God was blessing it, then the Holy Ghost and tongues are right; healing and the laying on of hands are right; praising God with the lifting up of hands is right; teaching the Word without majoring on the hooping is right. That's why many Baptist people resented my ministry and did not want to see me succeed beyond my father's level of success and worked hard to keep my ministry tied to him and the past. The bottom line was that they were not ready to change. What I was bringing back was different. Therefore, bringing my father up was symbolic of saying to me: **THE OLD IS BETTER** *(Luke 5:39)*. Once I realized that, his legacy was never a problem to me again.

It is amazing to me how traditional religious people always view things from an earthly human level. When I heard people make reference to the church as "my daddy's church," in my mind, I never saw it that way. Even when other churches and pastors referred to the church as being "Rev. So & So's" church, I always saw it as God's church. If I had seen it as a man's church or my father's church, then I would have been obligated to pastor it the way he did, and then build the church as a memorial unto him. I always had the ability and spiritual discernment to know the difference between honoring the Father of my spirit over the father of my flesh.

> *"Furthermore we have had fathers of our flesh which corrected us, and we have gave them reverence: **SHALL WE NOT MUCH RATHER BE IN SUBJECTION UNTO THE FATHER OF SPIRITS**, and live?"*
>
> *(Hebrews 12:9)*

Although, church people will not say it, the spirit of tradition will always elevate their leaders of the past over God.

In our old Lane Avenue sanctuary, there was a giant picture of my father that looked out over the auditorium. When you looked at it from any angle in the church it was as if he was looking at you. I knew the picture needed to come down, because the sanctuary ought to be a place where Jesus is the only focus, and no one else. Yet, it was another tradition in the black Baptist church to put the pastor's picture up in the sanctuary. I could see it being in the lobby of the church, but not in the area where our focus and attention should be on the Lord. I was trying to get the people to praise God and think on Him. When they opened their eyes while trying to think on Jesus, they saw Daddy.

I knew that if I bothered that picture and placed it in the vestibule area, there would be a problem - at least that's what I thought. Once again God intervened, and did it for me. The deacons came to me and told me the church sanctuary needed painting. This meant everything on the walls had to come down. The painters took the picture down, but did not put it back before they left. No one else came to me about putting it back up until after a while, no one even missed it or said anything about it. I ultimately had it put up in the front vestibule lobby area where it belonged.

What was so funny about it was I found out that there were many longtime members who felt the same way, but could not tell me, because it was my Dad. Satan will fight private wars in your mind that don't even exist. He had me thinking everyone would have a fit. I've seen Satan send one person in my office to express their dissatisfaction about something. That person knew how to interject, "Well everybody's saying…," "The people are saying…," or "They said…" Satan knows how to make **ONE SOUND LIKE 100**. Many times I stepped in the pulpit and fought battles that were not even there.

My desire was never to dishonor my father's memory or to cause the people to forget what he had done. He was one of the greatest men I ever knew. In 1984, I had the street - Lane Avenue renamed to J. W. Williams Lane. As previously mentioned, in each building we have purchased, the educational wing of the church has been dedicated to him to honor his love for helping many to have an education. A historical wall has been established to chronicle his work and the church's history in our present edifice and no matter where we go, I will always honor that.

I will always honor his work and will never allow the church to forget the work that he did. It is because of the Lord and him that I'm here today. As a matter of fact, another minister who knew my father in earlier years told me how my father told him that he would have made a change to a more Pentecostal ministry. He said that my father even considered the Church Of God In Christ, which at that time was probably the most well-known black Pentecostal denomination in the country. My father was one of the only few Baptist pastors in the city who would annually fellowship with the late Bishop J. O. Patterson, Sr., the presiding Bishop of the Church Of God In Christ at that time.

This pastor stated that my father told him that had he been a little younger, he would have made the change. I realized then that my transition was fulfillment of a call already established in my father. My father's generation did not have as much revelation of the Word as we do today. I was able to change because of the Copelands, Dr. Fred Price, and John Osteen that were on TV teaching revelation knowledge.

So he will never be forgotten. On the other side of the coin, his memory, nor anyone else's including mine after I am gone, should ever be exalted to the point that the people cannot move forward. I've worked hard to keep this in balance. I believe there is a normal place for remembering our past heritage and its leaders, yet not exalt them in our memory above Christ.

All I ever wanted was for my people to move forward with my leadership as I lead them into the new things of God. Psychologically, they could not do that as long as their hearts were in the past.

"REMEMBER YE NOT THE FORMER THINGS, NEITHER CONSIDER THE THINGS OF OLD. BEHOLD, I WILL DO A NEW THING; now it shall spring forth; shall ye not know it? I will even make a way in the wilderness, and rivers in the desert."

(Isaiah 43:18-19)

When we as a church began to move forward with God, He made a way through our wilderness of tradition and our dry desert of religion and brought us into rivers of living water through the Holy Ghost *(John 7:38)*. As I kept ministering the Word, God began to send others who were hungry. He gave me a new breed of people who were not bound to any loyalties of the past and free of past church "mess," mindsets, and issues.

CHANGING OLD MINDSETS

The growth was an answer to much prayer. I knew that most of the members from old Lane Avenue would not be able to mentally change. I knew their mindsets would be very difficult to break. Scripture proves this.

> *"And he spake also a parable unto them; **NO MAN PUTTETH A PIECE OF NEW GARMENT UPON AN OLD;** if otherwise, then both the new maketh a rent, and the piece that was taken out of the new agreeth not with the old. And no man putteth new wine into old bottles; else the new wine will burst the bottles, and be spilled, and the bottles shall perish. **BUT NEW WINE MUST BE PUT INTO NEW BOTTLES; AND BOTH ARE PRESERVED.** No man also having drunk old wine straightway desireth new: for he saith, **THE OLD IS BETTER.**"*
> ***(Luke 5:36-39)***

When I first got back from Tulsa, I felt like a new piece of denim material being stitched on an old pair of jeans. God had given me a new mindset based upon His Word. I was trying to give it to a people that felt the old was better. Although my church did not openly fight me in what I taught, I also knew the great majority of them would not be able to spiritually or mentally go with me where I was going. I had to have some new bottles that I could put this new wine in. People who were willing to change mentally, as some did, along with new people, who were coming in hungering for the new, were able to receive the new wine of the Spirit of God. I honor the members of old Lane Avenue who I started with that stayed with me through all of the change and transition.

They lost a lot. They lost their denominational foundation that they had been a part of all of their lives. They lost their church identity when the name was changed. They lost the closeness of a smaller church, but they stayed and many received the Word. They loved me enough not to openly fight me.

We have seen an increase in God's presence in our worship services, enrollment in Perfecting class has doubled, Helps Ministry participation has increased, and finances have gone up. He is the God of the hundredfold. I gave up or planted one church as a seed to God and God gave me three. We presently own and operate three church buildings, a radio station, two bookstores, a Christian Supper Club, and a Women's Outreach Ministry.

God has given me people for my life *(Isaiah 43:4)*. I have one of the greatest staffs a pastor could have. They are people who see, discern and are submitted to the vision.

THE WORD OF GOD, THE WORD OF GOD, THE WORD OF GOD, Pastors, is the key to changing your church. Keep pumping God's Word, speak the truth in love and let God's Word do the talking for you, and His Word will knock down every tradition that has been established by man. The Holy Ghost, if you allow Him in, will empower you and change the atmosphere of your local church *(Acts 1:8)*.

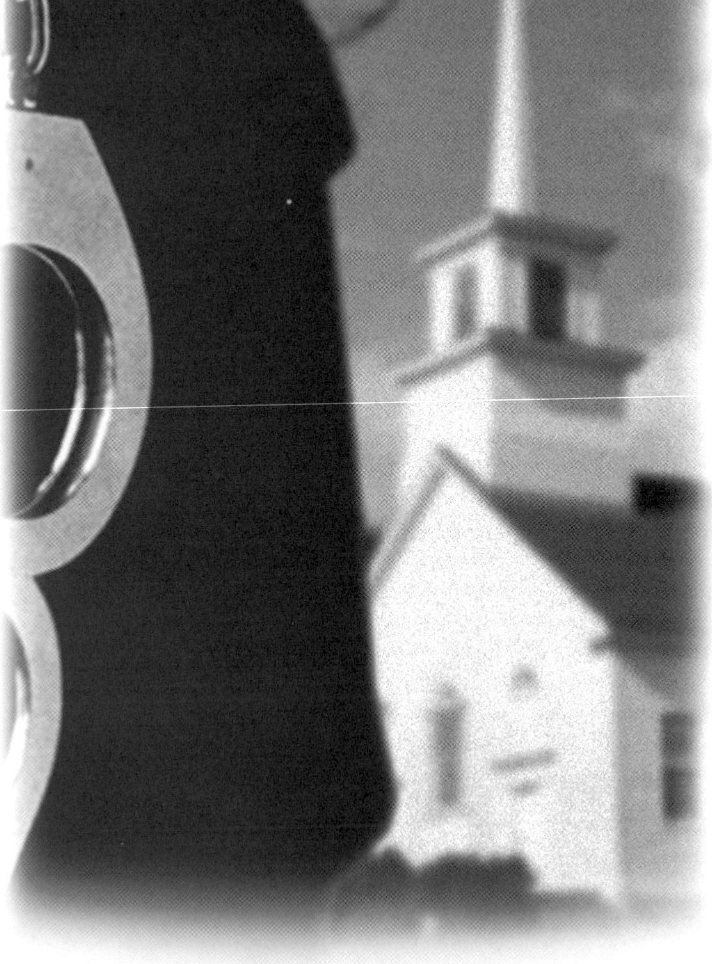

14

THE TEST FOR PASTORS

To the pastors who are reading this book, here is your *"acid"* test:
- Are you willing to endure a possible church split?
- Are you willing to endure the possible abandonment of members you love?
- Are you willing to possibly be fired from your church and have your salary cut off?
- Are you willing to be counted among the despised and ostracized?
- Are you willing to lose invitations to preach and have every door shut against you?
- Are you willing to be ridiculed and embarrassed because people look upon you as a fanatic?
- Are you willing to possibly lose the closeness and affection of your family?
- Are you willing to lose the prestige of your denominational standing?

If you cannot answer *"yes"* to all of these questions, then you may not be ready to make the step. Yes, you will lose the praise of men, but you will gain the praise of God over your ministry *(John 12:43)*. To this day men do not praise my ministry. Because of the increase and favor on my life and ministry however, is evident that I have the praise of God. Man will not bless your ministry. Man will not send you the people, money, building and resources you need to fulfill your ministry. But when you have the praise of God, **GOD WILL DO IT**.

YOU MAY HAVE TO START ANOTHER CHURCH

When the Spirit of God is upon your life, it may mean losing your church, but keep in mind, we have a Savior who has experienced the same rejection or who has been touched with the feeling of our infirmities *(Hebrews 4:15)*. He too, went to the traditional church of his day and tried to give them the Word of God, but they rejected Him and threw Him out of the church.

*"And Jesus returned in the power of the Spirit into Galilee: and there went out a fame of him through all the region round about. **AND HE TAUGHT IN THEIR SYNAGOGUES,** being glorified of all. And he came to Nazareth, where he had been brought up: and, as his custom was, he went into the synagogue on the Sabbath day, and stood up for to read. And there was delivered unto him the book of the prophet Esaias. And when he had opened the book, he found the place where it was written,"*

(Luke 4:14-17)

*"And all they in the synagogue, when they heard these things, **WERE FILLED WITH WRATH, AND ROSE UP, AND THRUST HIM OUT** of the city, and led him unto the brow of the hill whereon their city was built, that they might cast him down headlong."*

(Luke 4:28-29)

After they threw Jesus out of the church, what did Jesus do? He began to call a few disciples, or new bottles, and started another church *(Luke 5:10-11)*.

*"Nevertheless among the chief rulers also many believed on him; but **BECAUSE OF THE PHARISEES THEY DID NOT CONFESS HIM, LEST THEY SHOULD BE PUT OUT OF THE SYNAGOGUE: FOR THEY LOVED THE PRAISE OF MEN MORE THAN THE PRAISE OF GOD.**"*
(John 12:42-43)

THE FEAR OF PASTORS

Many pastors believe and know that there is more that God wants to do. They fear, however, being put out of the synagogue (church); they fear rocking the boat. They fear losing members; they fear losing money. They fear losing the fellowship of peers; they fear losing their positions and titles. Many preachers need the affirmation and approval of other men to validate their ministries. In order to preserve their reputations, they yield to receiving the praise of men rather than the praise of God. This is the danger of tradition.

You may not ever receive the love and accolades of man, but when God praises you in Heaven, He will exalt you and your ministry above anything that man could ever do. When God is pleased with you, He extends His praise by demonstrating and extending His favor to you.

I THANK GOD I AM A FREE MAN TODAY. Free to minister, preach and lead my people into the ways of God, without man's restraints.

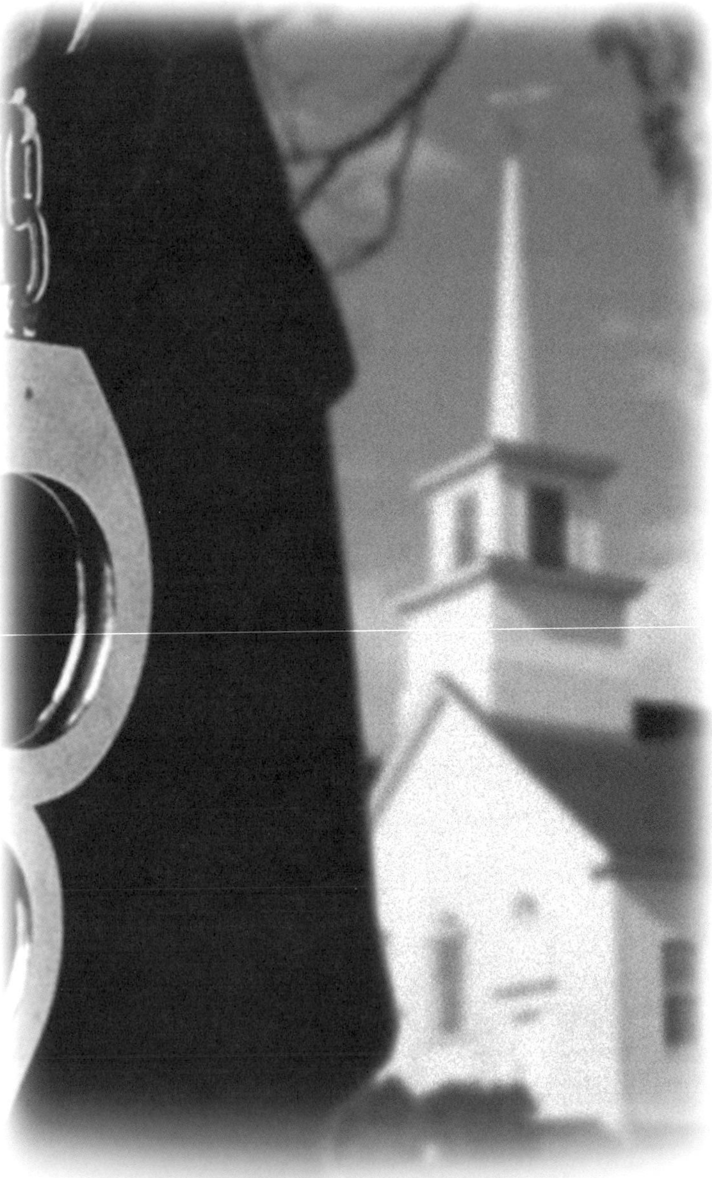

15

TRADITION AND THE WORD MOVEMENT

Prior to going to Rhema in 1987, I had begun listening to several Word Of Faith teachers on TV such as Dr. Fred Price, Kenneth Copeland, and John Osteen. These men, their books and TV programs made a big impact upon my life. It was through Dr. Fred Price that I learned about the teachings of Kenneth Hagin and Rhema Bible Training Center. Dr. Price had studied all of "Dad" Hagin's books and tapes and therefore, greatly influenced my decision to go to Tulsa.

During the 1970's, the Word of Faith movement somewhat intersected with Pentecostalism and advanced a break with the sanctified church tradition. The names just mentioned emerged as the Word of Faith pioneers. Dr. Fred Price was the pioneer for black Spirit-filled Word Christians. Word of Faith primarily rejected the anti-materialism (poverty) mentality of the sanctified church and saw financial prosperity as a Christian birthright along with salvation and healing. These leaders also introduced a new style of ministering the Word of God that countered the homiletic practices of the traditional church where they stressed instruction rather than inspiration. They specialize in introducing their congregations to the ways to access God's promises of health, wealth, and well-being by faith.

If you will notice, your independent, Spirit-filled Charismatic and/or Word ministries have individually had more impact on the world today than any one denomination. Denominations are tied to their traditions. They spend most of their time arguing over doctrine and rules and consequently, God cannot move. Men and women like Dr. Fred Price, Kenneth Copeland, Kenneth Hagin, Oral Roberts, John Osteen, Dr. Creflo Dollar, Bishop T. D. Jakes, Benny Hinn, Joyce Meyer and Marilyn Hickey have individually become bigger than any one denomination (with all its churches) by themselves. This one point alone proves that tradition makes the Word of God of none effect. These ministries have placed emphasis on exalting the Word of God.

The Word of God totally revolutionized my life and my thinking like never before. It exposed all of my old traditional belief systems. I saw God and life in a different way. I received revelation from the Word that brought freedom to my life. I now have a foundational working knowledge of the Word.

Yet, over the years, I began to see that many Word of Faith church groups and pastors, although not said, developed into a denominational mindset as well, with its own set of traditions. A denomination as defined by The American Heritage Dictionary, is nothing but *'a large group of religious congregations united under a common faith and name that becomes organized under a single administrative and legal hierarchy.'* Although each church carries its own autonomy, there is always the influence of the leadership. It is very difficult to stay in any group and not believe and preach what the leader preaches. If you are teaching anything else other than what the group's leader is teaching, you can be labeled a rebel. With any group you are going to be a part of, you are going to have to do like the group, in order to stay in it comfortably.

This is by no means an attack on the great faith teachers and generals such as the Hagins, the Copelands, Dr. Dollar, Dr. Price, John Osteen, Charles Capps, Norvel Hayes and others. These men of God have changed millions of lives and they have been very solid and balanced in their approach to the subject of faith.

My concern is two-fold in this chapter. First of all, there have been numerous pastors and teachers who have received the teaching of faith, but did not rightly divide it. A lot of false faith presumptions have been made. As a result, the message in many circles was not taught with balance and proper understanding.

Secondly, there are also many faith parishioners who have misunderstood and misapplied the principles of faith and consequently it has brought much confusion, condemnation, and legalism to the Body of Christ.

The Apostle Paul worked to keep the church walking in grace and faith, yet there were always those who advocated the letter of the law *(Galatians 2:16; 2 Corinthians 3:6)*. This is exactly what we have today in many Word circles.

I must admit God had to bring me to a place of balance and love. There were times in my early faith years that I saw myself walking with a puffed-up spirit *(1 Corinthians 8:1)*. Because of my lack of understanding, I made some big mistakes. This chapter is not designed to knock the Word of Faith message, it is only intended to bring clarity and balance. If we are not careful, the spirit of tradition will even creep into the circles of those who exalt the Word.

NO EMOTION

I believe one of the mistakes many Word churches have made was trying to change its image totally from what has been considered to be the "main line" traditional church. Although the traditional church world needed a shake up of its dry, stale religion and needed to be taught how to listen to the Word and not just react to antics and theatrics, the Word churches went totally from one extreme to the other. They took many things away, just because of its identity with the traditional church, and almost made some things a sin, not that God had called it sin. For example: the subject of emotions. Most of the black church world had been on the extreme left when it came to emotions. We used the hooping and hollering to raise people's emotions without giving them truth. The Word church came in and went to the other extreme: **WORD, WORD, WORD**. No emotion, no shouting, no response. I even heard some Word teachers say that if you hooped, raised your voice or hollered any, it was walking in death. In some Word churches, you were afraid to say *"Amen"* or *"Thank You Jesus"*, just to give witness to your agreement to the truth of the Word. I had to search for the balance. Some guys taught this because they just could not hoop or they had a more laid back style of ministry and personality. It was not their style, so they made their people feel like them because they did not hoop or did not like it. I know; I've been there and done that.

I almost made the mistake of trying to change what had been a traditional hooping, emotional church to a laid back, "don't-say-amen" church like what I had seen in the Word church circles. I learned, however, to adapt to my people. Any good fisherman will tell you that you have to change or adapt your fishing techniques to the fish. If the fish are not biting in a certain place, you either have to change your bait or put your line in the place or in a lower place where the fish are. I knew that if I was going to be the fisher of men that God had called me to be, I had to adapt to the fish and go to the level where they were in order to bring them up. The fisherman does not keep his line in the same place and just wait for the fish to come to him; he has to go where they are biting. I could not say, "OK, I've changed, y'all got to come up to my level." No, I had to meet them where they were, yet not compromise the truth. Paul said, **"And unto the Jews I became as a Jew, that I might gain the Jews;...I am made all things to all men that I might by all means save (or gain) some"** *(1 Corinthians 9:19-23).*

I had to give my people truth while I put a little "preach" in to make them want to bite. This had been a Baptist church for 45 years. It did not start out as a Charismatic Word church. Therefore, I had to adapt. The African-American pastors and people who came out of the traditional church learned their Charismatic Word worship style from the white Charismatic church. So when we came in looking for God, we found Him but we also adopted the white church culture with it, which usually had no emotion. Therefore, when we brought it into our churches, we totally killed anything that looked like the black church. If you were going to look like you were in the Spirit, you had to stand a certain way, hold your hands up a certain way, not with too much emotion. The songs had to be sung a certain way, in a certain style. It could not have any rhythmic beat, or the Spirit would not move. I agree that the words needed to be consistent with scripture, but it was almost as if our black heritage and style of worship was a "no-no." You ought to see some Spirit-filled African churches and watch how much emotion they expend in their worship. Listen to the rhythm and watch them dance. God made our people different from other nationalities. I will also have to admit that a lot of what was done in the traditional black church was performed in the flesh. I have found, however, that when we worship Him in Spirit and in truth, He can move in any church's worship culture *(John 4:23-24)*.

I had to distinguish between Word of Faith preachers' own personal preference, from what was God. I had to learn that just because some pastors chose a more laid back, no emotion, low-response type of service, that did not mean that I had to. I commend our early Word pioneers for taking black preachers out of their scripted pulpit sermons and bringing them down to where the people were and talking to them in a more intimate way. I learned to take my Bible and walk and talk to the people and minister directly to them from the Word. Yet, that has almost become a tradition in the Word church; because who said I can't stay at the podium sometimes if I want to? Although, there has never been a rule established about this, you come to realize that this is the flow and that's what you do to be in line with everybody else.

I praise God for men like Dr. Creflo Dollar, who is a faith teacher, but has brought balance to the message of faith. Dr. Dollar found a way to mix what he learned from his Word of Faith background, without totally abandoning some of the traditions of his African-American heritage. He teaches, but from time to time, he mixes in a little "preach." He also allows his choir to sing gospel music as long as it ministers the Word. The key once again, is balance and not going to the extreme on anything.

EXTREMES IN WORD OF FAITH TEACHING

There have even been many extremes in Word of Faith teaching. We have taught that God does not want you to be sick. If you are sick, you are not in the will of God or maybe you are in sin. True, sickness is not the will of God for us, but that does not mean that we will never be sick. We have heard faith teachers make statements like, "I will never be sick another day in my life." What happens is, if people get sick, they almost feel condemned. I remember being around some faith people and having a coughing type of cold. People who called themselves walking in faith, looked at me like I was something strange. No, it's the way it has been taught. Sickness is not God's will, which lets me know I have the right to resist and come against this thing. So if you get sick, take the Word of God and stand against it and do not feel condemned.

We also led people to believe that if you had to use doctors or medicine, something was wrong with your faith. A lot of people would be dead were it not for doctors *(2 Chronicles 16:12)*. Yet, the balance is not to put all your trust in doctors, but there are times the Bible teaches using the means of man or what God placed in the earth for our healing. Why didn't Paul tell Timothy to use his faith for stomach problems instead of wine *(1 Timothy 5:23)*? Hezekiah was told by the man of God to use a plaster for his boil instead of using faith *(Isaiah 38:21)*. **THERE IS BALANCE**. Go to the doctor, use your medication, yet learn how to apply the Word of God and your faith at the same time.

WORRY

I heard teachings that said, "I will never be worried or depressed another day in my life." That may be the experience of some who have come to a certain point of maturity. Most Christians, however, will never come to that point. I have also grown to where I am no longer a chronic worrier and depressed, as I used to be. Yet, there are times

I have been faced with a circumstance where I had to resist and stand against depression, and because I had heard other faith teachers say they never worried, I felt condemned when I did not measure up to their standards. Thank God, that if I do get depressed, the Word has given me the legal right to come out of it. If I had taught the extreme and not given people the room to make mistakes and overcome human weaknesses, I probably would have no church today.

WHEN BAD THINGS HAPPEN

We taught that nothing bad could ever come from God. Everything that looked bad to us had to come from the devil. There are some things, however, on our end that may look bad, but is actually from God for our good. God will shake up things in our lives or break up certain relationships for our good, in order to keep us on the road to our destiny *(Hebrews 12:26-27)*. To us it looks like it is Satan, so we start rebuking and binding the devil. Sometimes, when our hearts are filled with pride, God has to allow or do things that will humble our hearts.

> *"Likewise, ye younger, submit yourselves unto the elder. Yea, all of you be subject one to another, and be clothed with humility: for* **GOD RESISTETH THE PROUD,** *and giveth grace to the humble."*
> *(1 Peter 5:5)*

The word *"resist"* in this passage means to oppose or stand against. God actually opposes and stands against us when we are in pride. Yet, we are confessing the Word to change circumstances without first changing our hearts.

> *"And thou shalt remember all the way which* **THE LORD THY GOD LED THEE** *these forty years in the wilderness,* **TO HUMBLE THEE, AND TO PROVE THEE, TO KNOW WHAT WAS IN THINE HEART,** *whether thou wouldest keep his commandments, or no.*

AND HE HUMBLED THEE, and SUFFERED THEE TO HUNGER, and fed thee with manna..."

(Deuteronomy 8:2-3)

God allowed them or caused them (whatever you want to say), to be hungry in order to humble them and to prove their hearts. God will put us in situations to see if we will keep His commandments. God not only allowed, but He caused an uncomfortable situation for Israel such as being without food to test their hearts. Satan does not want to test us to see if we will keep God's commandments.

ABIDING IN THE WORD

We taught confessing the Word, but did not emphasize abiding in Him and letting the Word abide in us *(John 15:7)*. Therefore, we would pick up the Bible and find a few promises, quote them a couple of times, and close the Bible up. We never spent time with the God of the Word. If we are not careful, we can make a god out of the Word and overlook the God of the Word. Confessing the Word can become a ritual of works where we learn to depend on our ability to speak the Word enough times, rather than learn how to place childlike faith and trust in God with our confessing.

We have used the Word to promote our agendas and order our lives in the way we want them to go rather than seek God for His plan and purpose. There is not much encouragement to spend time seeking God in many Word churches. Why? Because you've got the Word. Get the promise from the Word and that's all you need. Yet, the Bible says faith and seeking God are synonymous:

*"But without **FAITH** it is impossible to please him: for he that cometh to God must believe that he is, and that he is a rewarder of them that **DILIGENTLY SEEK HIM.**"*

(Hebrews 11:6)

HELPING THE POOR

We have not helped the poor or given to the poor as we should have because all they need to do is get the Word and stand on it like I did to get what they need from God. If I got mine, get yours. This was the unspoken attitude that existed.

*"He that **HATH PITY UPON THE POOR LENDETH UNTO THE LORD;** and that which he hath given will he pay him again."*
*(**Proverbs 19:17**)*

DELIVERANCE FROM DEMONS

The Word church was somewhat quiet on the subject of demons and deliverance. We were taught that if you need to cast the devil out, use the Word and take authority. This will work for some. There are many people, however, who have never moved to that level of faith. If a person's mind is being oppressed by the devil and they need deliverance, they don't have the stability of mind to stand on the Word. Oppression from demons can keep some people so confused until they can't pray or read the Word.

Jesus did not say in *Mark 16:18* to just stand on the Word or use faith to deal with demons. He said: **CAST THEM OUT.** We have overlooked the effectiveness of balanced deliverance ministry, and Jesus spent most of His ministry confronting evil spirits. It was also the first thing He commissioned His disciples to do when He sent them out *(Matthew 10:1)*.

Although, there have been some extremes and abuses in many of today's deliverance ministries, there still is room for balanced, valid deliverance ministry. This will be one of the church's priorities as we move closer to the return of the Lord. More and more people will be coming to our churches who have been involved in all kinds of occultic, idolatrous practices and will need to be set free. The world is slowly becoming a habitation of devils *(Revelation 18:2,23)*.

There are people in many Word churches who are dealing with demons still lodged in the area of their souls, not in their spirits. Those demon spirits have never been driven out from things they were involved in, in the past. There are curses, although legally broken through Jesus' work on the cross, have not been broken experientially. Therefore, many are under the delusion that just because they are filled with the Holy Ghost, there is no way they can have a demon. Most do not, yet it is not impossible.

People think that because our bodies are the temple of God and the Holy Ghost dwells in our spirits, there cannot be any spirits of darkness inside our souls. God parallels our bodies with His temple buildings. Remember, even Jesus had to whip or cast the evil moneychangers out of God's temple while the Spirit of God was dwelling in the Holy of Holies. That presence did not stop evil people from serving their evil desires in the inner court area of that temple *(Mark 11:15-17)*.

We recently tried to minister to a young woman from a Word church who had cancer. She claimed she had been standing on the Word, but there had been no change. We offered her an opportunity to receive deliverance, but she could not accept the fact that she was possibly dealing with a spirit. She was Holy Ghost-filled, and this was not in line with the traditional teachings of her Word church. She died in her late thirties.

The danger of being locked into any group with its own set of teachings is that it can keep you from being open to what the Spirit of God might give you outside of what the group thinks or teaches. I've learned how to fellowship with various groups, receive what I can from them, and yet stay open and always be led by the Spirit in terms of what God's plan is for my church as well as for me individually.

To admit that there is demonic oppression in our lives means we have got to confess or acknowledge that we have a problem somewhere. People who adhere to faith teaching think that they have to believe that there is no problem. Only confess what the Word of God says. We go around saying, "I'm not believing or confessing that." So rather than acknowledge and deal with a problem, we go on pretending that there is none *(James 5:16; 1 John 1:9)*.

MY CONFESSION TO THE CHURCH

In 1998, after being on about a month-long sabbatical, I came back to the church one Sunday morning and made an open confession to the entire congregation that my wife and I had been having some marital problems for a while and that we had argued over and over while I was out. I told them how I didn't have it altogether like I thought I did. It was like a weight lifted from my shoulders. For the first time I was transparent about something very personal to me. Right there in the service, I began to cry, weep and repent before the people.

Yes, I was afraid that I might be viewed by some as not walking in the faith that I had taught. Yes, I feared that someone would say, "Pastor, you've been teaching us to have faith and live right in our homes, how come it's not working for you." Yet, to my surprise when I owned up to my shortcomings, my people began to weep also. Many came to the altar and repented themselves. I saw other husbands bring their wives to the altar repenting to God and to their spouse. An atmosphere of repentant worship took place that day. Afterwards many people called to thank me for being open because it caused them to deal with themselves. Some told me how they had been trying to live up to this perfect faith standard in their marriage and when they made mistakes, they felt condemned. Yet, when I opened up, it gave them hope for their marriages.

That day, faith's religious mask came off. This is not to say that faith does not work. However, we must give people the room and freedom to grow and make mistakes without condemnation; and as pastors, we must be transparent about our own shortcomings as we develop in faith.

The Word church anointing wave was intended to be God's army gathering to be trained. God took a remnant people out of the denominations and formed a people that would be a praise to Him in the earth. The army has been gathered and trained and now its time to take the message that we have learned to the lost which is God saves, heals, delivers, and prospers. The church, however, is still lavishing in its material things and not doing kingdom work.

A LACK OF TOLERANCE

I saw a lack of tolerance for those who we felt were weaker in faith than we *"Word people"* were. I remember, before changing the name of our church, going to a Word conference and there was a roll call of the churches present. After all the claps went up for all the "Christian Center, Faith Fellowship, and Word of Faith" churches, they called our name, "Lane Avenue Baptist Church," and no one said a word. The expression was, "What are they doing here?" There was always a bashing of all denominational churches, particularly Baptist. When you are around that, you begin to do it as well. I've had to repent before God many times for my spiritual arrogance and pride, because this was not the spirit of Jesus. God taught me how to deal with the spirit of tradition and religion and not the church itself.

"Him that is **WEAK IN THE FAITH RECEIVE YE,** *but not to doubtful disputations."*

(Romans 14:1)

There is a point to where it is good to expose religion and tradition. Jesus definitely did it *(Matthew 23)*.

When you use the name Baptist or Methodist as a whole, however, it places all churches of that name in the same category and as I said earlier, there are many denominational churches moving into the things of God. God had to teach me how to **ATTACK THE SPIRIT OF RELIGION AND TRADITION** and not the people or the denomination as a whole *(Ephesians 6:12)*.

God showed me that what we were doing was trying to elevate ourselves above others. The more we talked other churches down, the more it would make us appear to be better in the eyes of people. We bolstered our spiritual knowledge and pride in the event our people were tempted to go back to their old denominational churches *(1 Corinthians 8:1)*. No matter how much spiritual knowledge we receive, if it is not mixed with love, *"I am become as sounding brass or a tinkling cymbal" (1 Corinthians 13:1)*.

DEALING WITH GRIEF

I also had to balance my thinking on the issue of grief. There is excessive grief when people become depressed or almost suicidal at the loss of a loved one, which is what we must stay away from. I believe there is a place in God, however, for going through the process of healthy grief, when we are no longer with a person. Paul said: *"Sorrow not as them which have no hope." (1 Thessalonians 4:13)* God did not say we could not sorrow, but not to sorrow as the people of the world who have no hope beyond this life.

At some Word churches, when you go to a funeral, you are afraid to cry or show any sorrow. I am so glad that Jesus was willing to show emotion when he wept *(John 11:35)*. Regardless to what He was crying about, He still was not so spiritual that He could not shed a tear. ***"WEEPING MAY ENDURE FOR A NIGHT, BUT JOY COMETH IN THE MORNING** (Psalm 30:5)*. I am so glad that even though some faith teachers won't allow me to cry, Jesus does. He acknowledged and respected human emotions.

Verily, verily, I say unto you, **THAT YE SHALL WEEP AND LAMENT,** *but the world shall rejoice: and* **YE SHALL BE SORROWFUL,** *but your sorrow shall be turned into joy.*

(John 16:20)

PRODUCING HARD COLD ROBOTS

The tragedy of many Word people is that we are producing hard, cold, robotic converts. People are afraid to be human beings who can admit weaknesses yet, learn how to receive God's grace and patiently learn to overcome them without a sense of condemnation. We have made a law almost out of not speaking wrong words and not admitting the truth about ourselves *(2 Corinthians 3:6)*. We have shouted, "Let the weak say I'm strong"; never say that you are weak. Even the Apostle Paul was willing to acknowledge and confess that He and us, as the Body of Christ, have to deal with weaknesses:

> *"And he said unto me, My grace is sufficient for thee: for my strength is made perfect in* **WEAKNESS.** *Most gladly therefore will I rather glory in my infirmities, that the power of Christ may rest upon me. Therefore I take pleasure in infirmities, in reproaches, in necessities, in persecutions, in distresses for Christ's sake: for* **WHEN I AM WEAK,** *then am I strong."*
>
> *(2 Corinthians 12:9-10)*

> *"For though he was crucified through weakness, yet he liveth by the power of God. For* **WE ALSO ARE WEAK** *in him, but we shall live with him by the power of God toward you. For we are glad,* **WHEN WE ARE WEAK,** *and ye are strong: and this also we wish, even your perfection."*
>
> *(2 Corinthians 13:4,9)*

People are trying to look and act the part in front of their faith pastors or fellow faith members, and yet behind the scenes they are hurting. We have established an environment where people do not have the freedom to say,

"I'm hurting or I'm failing in this area", or "I don't have it all together like I thought I did." So they begin to play this faith role to measure up. They begin to use their little knowledge to act as if they know it all, when in actuality their lives do not show any fruit or evidence of the knowledge they claim to have. All of the "Praise God brother," and "I'm blessed of the Lord and highly favored," at some point should show in your life. Jesus said to let your light shine before men. He criticized the Pharisees for their religious jargon and expressions to try to prove spirituality *(Matthew 6:5-8)*.

THE SUBJECT OF DEATH

On the subject of death, there were teachings that taught we can live until we are 120 years of age *(Genesis 6:3)*. I'm not saying that this cannot happen or be attained, however, there are so many factors involved in this happening that most people will never reach that. Think of the spiritual, mental, emotional, and physical discipline involved: eating right, getting adequate rest, no stress, discipline in the Word, discipline in prayer, continuously walking in love, living holy, obedience in every area and talking right. Most Christians will never walk in this kind of discipline.

When people have died before they were 70, we said that they must have been in sin. I do believe Christians have the right to believe God for long life *(Proverbs 3:2)*. Too many Christians are dying before their time *(Ecclesiastes 7:17)*. Yet, this may not be the case for all Christians *(Isaiah 57:1-2)*. Some Christians will be made martyrs *(Revelation 2:13)*. Also I believe completed purpose will determine when we leave this earth *(Ephesians 1:9-11)*. If we do not fulfill purpose or if purpose has been fulfilled, will determine when we leave this earth.

I remember talking to a so-called "faith person." I have found that some people just want to act spiritual to try to show what they know when in actuality they are really puffed up. In the conversation, I was sharing an experience where I was frightened about something. I made a statement that ended with, "like to have scared me to death." If you had seen her expression, you would have thought that I had cursed. She said, "Oh brother, don't say that or death will come." I will admit, we do need to be careful about our words concerning death. If you start believing and talking about not living long or dying early, it is possible that you can speak death over your life.

This woman, however, acted as if a lightning bolt was about to strike me over something I said with the intent of being humorous at the moment. The principle of faith according to *Mark 11:23* involves saying, believing and not doubting, which means in order for your faith to work; in order for your words to have impact, you must say it and believe it in your heart. Without belief in the heart concerning what you say, the principle of faith cannot work. Your words only have impact when there is belief. Therefore, when I made the statement, "scared me to death," I was not believing in my heart that I was going to actually die. My words had no belief behind them. Once again, let's have some balance with faith and speaking words and not get into bondage.

SIN CONSCIOUSNESS

We taught that you cannot receive from God by faith if you are "sin-conscious." This is true. If you are always thinking about all the things you have done wrong in the past and feeling guilty over those things, you will not receive. Your faith will not work. We never stressed the importance of repentance, however, over the junk that is actually present in our lives. Nine times out of ten it's that junk that's blocking the blessing. It is important and balanced to teach a lifestyle of daily repentance yet, moving on and not staying in condemnation when we sin. **REPENTANCE BEFORE FAITH** *(Mark 1:15).*

We are trying so desperately to help people be in a position to have faith and receive from God until we are missing some very basic spiritual principles. We are trying so hard to help them see themselves as God sees them.

Consequently, people are ignoring their present heart condition. They are ignoring sin totally, which means we are preaching to a bunch of folk in all kinds of ungodly heart conditions and lifestyles. When people are in rebellion, lust, and disobedience, their minds and conscience will be defiled and therefore, it will affect their faith. When people's hearts are impure, their desires will be impure.

"Unto the pure all things are pure: but unto ***THEM THAT ARE DEFILED AND UNBELIEVING IS NOTHING PURE;*** *but even* ***THEIR MIND AND CONSCIENCE IS DEFILED."***

(Titus 1:15)

That's why it is of the utmost importance that we teach people more about repentance and keeping their hearts right so that they can be in a position to receive from God.

If the prophets, Jesus, Paul and the other apostles preached against sin; if the Bible deals with sin and did not ignore it, then we too must do the same thing. I'm afraid to say it, but we have developed a doctrine that has caused people to totally ignore sin, or the real issues going on in their lives just so they can receive from God. I'm not saying that this is how all faith teachers are teaching it, but this is definitely how many faith people are perceiving it.

TAKE CARE

I remember how you couldn't tell someone in parting to "take care." I told a faith person one day to "take care" as we were leaving. She said, "I don't receive that brother, because I've given all of my cares to the Lord." I wanted to say, "You faith fool, I'm not telling you to take care (or be anxious and worried or overly concerned about your problems kind of care)." This kind of care from *1 Peter 5:7* is found in Strong's Greek Dictionary #3308 which means to be distracted. When I'm telling someone to "take care," I am not saying to worry or be distracted; I'm saying take normal, practical care of yourself, be watchful and vigilant of what's going on around you, drive safely. There is nothing wrong with that. Even Jesus used the expression "take care" in the Good Samaritan parable:

> *"And on the morrow when he departed, he took out two pence, and gave them to the host, and said unto him, **TAKE CARE** of him; and whatsoever thou spendest more, when I come again, I will repay thee."*
> **(Luke 10:35)**

If it was good enough for Jesus, it is good enough for me.

THE MEMBER WHO ALMOST DIED

Finally, I guess the one experience that brought balance to my teaching more than anything else was in the early 90's at the conclusion of one of our New Year's Eve Services. One of our longtime members had an aneurysm. She was rushed to the hospital and almost died, but we travailed and prayed that night like never before, and God spared her life. It was told to me by one of her family members that she had stopped taking her blood pressure medication saying that she was healed. I knew then she called herself trying to have faith. Although I never taught my members to stop taking their medication, some people analyzed that if they were still taking the medicine, it must mean they didn't have faith.

I had to look at some of her unsaved family members as they looked at me with disdain in that hospital waiting room. I knew they were blaming me for what they thought I was teaching. Yet, I inwardly took the blame that maybe I didn't stress enough continuing to take medication as your faith builds.

One of the things that was never made clear or stressed in Word circles was the importance of abiding in the Word through meditation. The Word has to become engrafted or rooted in our hearts *(James 1:21)*. Most people take the Word of Faith teacher's word for it or make a few confessions that they are healed, but they are never willing to put in the time to get that word grounded never receive a revelation or rhema word on healing. Therefore, it has become only a me__ that's not good enough. If that Word is not engrafted in your spirit, you are going to die if you have a terminal illness.

I am a faith man, don't get me wrong. I believe in speaking the Word and standing on the Word, but I thank God for balance. I had to do like the Berean Christians and not take somebody else's word for it, but be diligent and study the Word for myself *(Acts 17:10-11)*. Speaking the Word keeps your spirit built up.

THE DESIRES OF OUR HEART

We were also taught that we could have the desires of our heart. So if we saw a particular house that we desired, we began believing and confessing for it. No matter how much resistance there was to it, we kept on believing, because that's the one we want. I have since learned to also seek the wisdom and will of God in a situation *(James 1:5)*. Yes, it is His will that my need is met to have a house, but that house may not be God's best. So I've learned to believe God for something and yet add a postscript to my faith:

> "God, I like this house and I desire it, but I respect your wisdom. You may have something better for me that I cannot see. If this house is not the one that you have for me or is not the best one, if there is something about this house that's bad for me and I cannot see it, you block it for me."

This is important because our spirits and souls are so close, the Bible says it has to be divided asunder *(Hebrews 4:12)*. Sometimes our desires are coming from our selfish souls, which are governed by our minds and emotions and we can sometimes think it's God. The spirit man is led by the Holy Ghost. Let's face it, sometimes we are not always hearing clearly, our spirits are not always as sensitive as they need to be; so when I give respect to the wisdom of God, I am humbling myself to whatever His best is for my life and not being lead by my own possible selfish desires.

DON'T OVERLOOK GOD'S PURPOSE

I've also learned the importance of purpose. Some things are going to happen because we are in line with God's predestined plan for our lives *(Ephesians 1:11)*. There have been things that I have received from God that I did no confession for or anything on my own. God just did it, because it was in line with His purpose for my life.

Sometimes just plain old obedience will bring the blessings of God *(Isaiah 1:19; Job 36:11)*. I've seen ministers trying to believe God for a specific number of members that they were never purposed by God to have. God has not graced or gifted everyone to have 18,000 or 25,000 members *(Matthew 25:15)*. Seek God's plan and purpose for your life and it will help to channel your faith properly.

THANK GOD FOR THE WORD OF FAITH

Once again, let me be clear. I thank God for my Word of Faith background. We needed the teaching of faith to bring us out of the dungeons of religion. We needed to know that God loved us and wanted to heal and prosper us. We needed to have our distorted image of who God is and who we are corrected, so we can see Him for who He truly is and position ourselves to come to Him boldly without condemnation.

We needed the Word movement to bring us to God so that He could become our passion and not the things of this world *(Colossians 3:2)*. Too much of Word teaching today is still being consumed on the believer and the things of this earth: prosperity, wealth, who we are in Christ, miracles, being blessed, speaking to **OUR** mountains, the authority of the **BELIEVER**. Yes, I believe and teach those things too, but what happened to just a good old-fashioned intimate relationship and fellowship with Jesus? What happened to just loving Him and getting His heart for the world and not my heart? Whatever happened to the desire for seeing souls come into the kingdom? What happened to just *"seek ye first the kingdom"* and let God automatically add these things to our lives *(Matthew 6:33)?* We've lost something.

Most members in Word churches came from denominational churches where they were already saved. Even though our membership numbers have looked good to people, it still has not made a dent in the kingdom of darkness. Our ministries are still not appealing to the lost. I will not be satisfied until I see an abundance of unsaved souls come into the church like they did on the day of Pentecost after Peter preached. That's when I will know that my teaching has reached the level of impact as the bible apostles.

There are many sound teachings of the Word movement that have produced great results in my life. I have seen the Word of God bring healings, peace of mind, joy, answered prayers and personal deliverances to my life. I've seen Satan have to flee, because of the revelation I received on the authority that I have as a believer. I've seen God prosper my life and ministry through faith in His Word. Yet, I believe the church has gotten off course from God's original intent and plan, because of our overemphasis on faith and material things. Our focus has become a self-centered lifestyle, and we have lost our first love, which is Him *(Revelation 2:4)*. Our emphasis has become the things and what belongs to us instead of Jesus. Now that we know who we are, let's go after God.

A RICH LUKEWARM CHURCH

God gives us a prophetic message for today's church in *Revelation 3:14-21*. John writes letters to the seven (7) churches in Asia. Scholars believe that each church is representative of a particular age or period in the church's 2,000-year history. The church of Laodicea is the last church, which means this is the condition of the church before the rapture comes. In *Chapter 4*, we see that the

Lord is no longer speaking. *Verse 1* speaks of hearing a trumpet and John was told to "come up hither." Thessalonians talks about a trumpet blowing when we are raptured and caught up *(1 Thessalonians 4:16)*. Therefore, what you see going on in Laodicea, the last church, at the end of the church age, is indicative of what is going on in the church today.

> *"And unto the angel of the church of the Laodiceans write; These things saith the Amen, the faithful and true witness, the beginning of the creation of God; I know thy works, that* **THOU ART NEITHER COLD NOR HOT:** *I would thou wert* **COLD OR HOT.** *So then because thou art* **LUKEWARM,** *and neither cold nor hot, I will spue thee out of my mouth. Because thou sayest,* **I AM RICH, AND INCREASED WITH GOODS, AND HAVE NEED OF NOTHING; AND KNOWEST NOT THAT THOU ART WRETCHED, AND MISERABLE, AND POOR, AND BLIND, AND NAKED."*
>
> *(Revelation 3:14-17)*

God has to be talking to the Charismatic Word church because the traditional church world, as well as the sanctified, Pentecostal church has never had a revelation of being rich, wealthy, or prosperous.

The church is lukewarm towards God and has lost its passion and zeal for Him *(verse 19)*. Why? We are stuck teaching only what benefits the believer. We have become rich and increased with material things and have come to the place that we have need of nothing. Yet, the Word church is not aware of how spiritually bankrupt it has become. We have used blessings and material things as a badge to prove to others that everything is alright with us and God. "Hey, if I got a new house, car and job that I believed God for, me and God must be alright." He would not bless me unless I had it altogether.

This scripture proves that it is possible to have the blessings and the things, yet be miserable spiritually and inwardly or not right with God. I believe Satan and his demons will sometimes take some of their resistance away if it will help them achieve a higher purpose of pulling Christians away from God. He will let stuff come through for you if he senses that you are a candidate for being lukewarm.

Isn't that what tradition does? It uses the external things to prove spirituality as opposed to the internal issues of the heart. What was Jesus' remedy? **REPENT!** *(Revelation 3:19)* God is calling all of His churches today to **REPENT!**

IT'S CALLED GOD'S CHURCH, NOT A FAITH CHURCH

I had a faith teacher come and minister at my church about a year ago. He stated that our church should be a *"faith"* church. What he meant was a faith church "as they were," a faith church. We are a church that believes in faith and preaches faith, but I'd just rather be God's church. When you say you are a "faith church," it means that faith is the emphasis of your church. There are too many facets of God's kingdom message other than faith.

Our church believes in faith, evangelism, deliverance, prophecy, prosperity, holiness, prayer, healing, and spiritual warfare, but none of these are overemphasized. They are all ingredients that go into making up God's church. I did not want to be labeled a faith church, a deliverance church, a holiness church, or a prophecy church. Yet, I believe and preach all of these things.

Too often we have succumbed to focusing our attention on one aspect of Jesus' teaching rather than developing a relationship with the Teacher. This misplaced focus has lead to all kinds of church movements and denominations that divide and weaken us. All of the aforementioned areas of focus are valid and necessary aspects of the Christian life, but all too often these teachings become the filter by which we define our Christian lives. Instead, we must constantly keep the plumb line of simple devotion to Him. If we allow ourselves to get stuck on a "pet" teaching or doctrine, we will end up on the road to inward fruitlessness *(Revelation 3:17)* and outward powerlessness. If we do not have these times of intimacy and truly experiencing Him, then anything – our ministry, our theology, and all of our good church activities can easily become idols; keeping us from a deep relationship with the very One we are serving.

IT'S ABOUT JESUS AND HIM ALONE

In conclusion, I have come full circle through man's denominations and church movements. I have been born and raised a Baptist, I've seen the Pentecostal Holiness churches; I've been in Charismatic circles; I've studied and taught Word of Faith principles; I helped to birth the Full Gospel Baptist Church Fellowship; I've learned from and sat at the feet of some of God's greatest men: Rev. Jasper Williams, Sr. & Jr., Dr. Frederick Price, Kenneth Hagin, John Osteen, Bishop Paul Morton, and Dr. Creflo Dollar. It has taken me 23 years of ministry to finally come to the realization that it's Jesus and Him alone.

When you have been touched by His glory, it will transform your values and perception of life. Man's traditions, positions, and titles don't matter anymore. Yes, I have the faith to believe God for a new Mercedes or a house, but I would rather focus my faith and energies on seeing 10,000 people come to Jesus in one night. Material blessings and provisions are nice and God is not against that, but when your heart has been transformed by God's glory, you long for His presence. I've grown to love and desire the things my Master loves and desires. The things of the earth instantly grow dim in comparison to Him.

I believe we have clearly entered into the post-Charismatic Word era or wave of anointing. Faith will always be needed. All of God's principles must be propelled by faith and prosperity is the will of God. Jesus and souls, however, has to become our emphasis. We are beginning to see the first droplets of that new wave of anointing and glory, called the great harvest of the Lord. **REVIVAL IS IN THE LAND.**

We have entered the new end-time Apostolic age where God is having to restore last what He intended to be first. Because of the traditions of men, the church has been blinded to the reality of this valuable church building and church-reforming gift *(1 Corinthians 12:28; Ephesians 4:11-12).* The Word ministries have taught the body. Now God is raising up Apostles with a mission to mobilize and unify the church to go to war. The era of superstar TV evangelist ministry is over. We have entered the era of the saints in the pews being the stars in the trenches, doing Kingdom battle. Apostles have a three-fold purpose:

1. *Reform the religious systems of men.*
2. *Prepare the church for the end-time harvest.*
3. *And foremost, lead the body back to intimacy and relationship with Jesus.*

Another tradition that has been taught is that Apostles were primarily missionaries sent to foreign lands to plant churches. They are not primarily needed in America because there are churches everywhere. When you think about how dry the land is of properly built churches on a solid biblical foundation, as well as churches that need to be reformed, it is no wonder we have entered into the new apostolic reformation age. When new non-traditional churches are established and old ones are reformed, God will have somewhere to send His coming end-time harvest.

The apostolic leaders who are coming forth will not be identified by their association to any particular group or denomination. Paul was not a part of Jesus' original group of twelve. His call was not based on their approval or knowledge. Apostolic ministry cannot be limited to any one group or denomination. God chooses and calls whom He desires. **THE WALL OF TRADITION MUST FALL!**

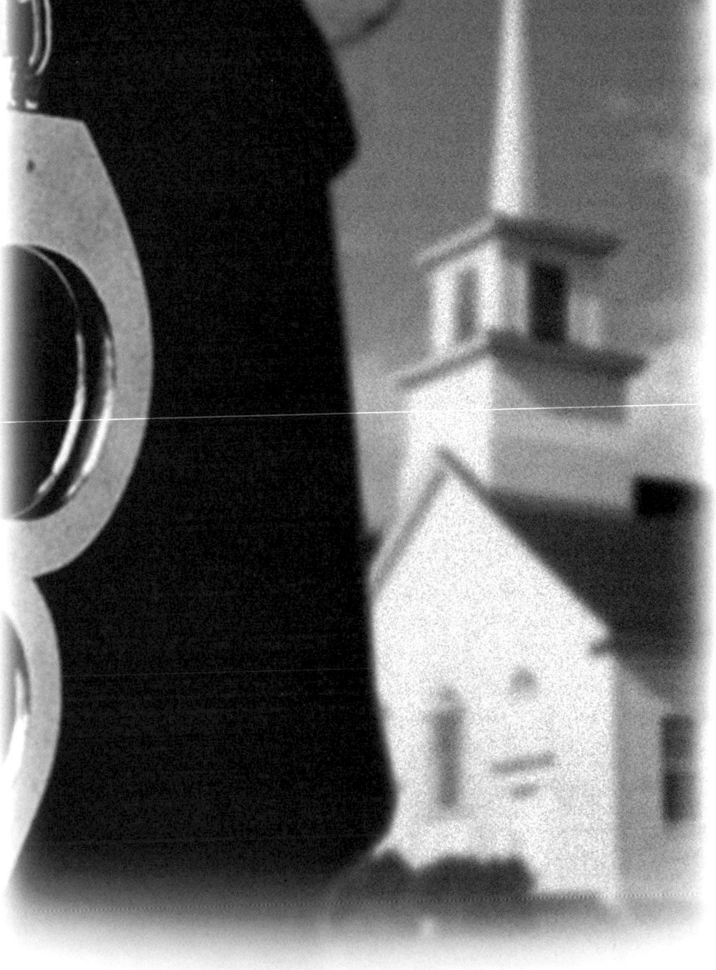

16

DESTINY FOUND

In 1996, God gave a prophetic word to me through Prophet Kevin Leal (at that time of Tulsa, OK). The Spirit of God placed an Apostolic call upon my life and the ministry of our church. This was reconfirmed by Apostle John Eckhardt in December of 1999. I accepted the call in September 2000 with an official consecration and ordination service.

An apostle is one called and sent by Christ to have the spiritual authority, character, gifts and abilities to successfully reach and establish people in kingdom truth and order, especially through planting and overseeing local churches. Apostolic people are Christians who support and participate in apostolic ministry, but are not actual apostles. They work with apostles to reach the lost through dynamic outreach, church planting and nurturing.

One of the main jobs of the apostle is to bring reformation and challenge the status quo religious systems of the church. The apostle brings the church into biblical order. They uproot old religious foundations and establish new biblical foundations. They establish proper church government according to the Word of God; they are defenders of the faith and truth; they enforce kingdom conduct, righteousness, holiness, and obedience; they bring revelation and understanding to the church. The work of the apostle is beyond the local church; he is to touch his city for the kingdom of God. They train their people to do the work of the ministry, etc. and so much more.

After years of searching, I finally found my destiny. When I studied books on the office of the apostle, I understood why I always had a resistance in my spirit against tradition. I was never a conformist to the status quo religious system. Like Jeremiah, God had already sanctified and ordained me before I entered into my mother's womb to be an Apostle of the Lord Jesus Christ.

I tried to fit into the traditional ministerial role, but God had another plan for my life – to raise up kingdom churches and establish them on biblical kingdom order. My destiny has been found. Had I continued to walk in the traditions of men and closed my mind to biblical truth, I would have never found my destiny, purpose and assignment.

Finally, I have had several pastors to ask me, "How did you get to where you are?" "What was your secret?" and "What are you doing?" My response is, "I only did what the Bible said." Remember, Jesus promised the hundredfold to those who were willing to leave it all for His sake and the Gospel. People are trying to only give their way or speak their way into the hundredfold. Jesus said it comes when you are willing to release all to follow Him. That means whatever stands in your way to keep you from obeying Him and fully following Him: family, position, ambition, personal goals, job, career, business, money, houses, land, or the desires of people. I will say it again, if you can give it up, you can have it all *(Matthew 19:27-30)*.

Let me conclude by praying for you one of Paul's many epistle prayers:

> *"THAT THE GOD OF OUR LORD JESUS CHRIST, the Father of glory, MAY GIVE unto YOU THE SPIRIT OF WISDOM and REVELATION IN THE KNOWLEDGE OF HIM: The EYES OF YOUR UNDERSTANDING BEING ENLIGHTENED; THAT YE MAY KNOW WHAT IS THE HOPE OF HIS CALLING, and what the riches of the glory of his inheritance in the saints."*
>
> ***(Ephesians 1:17-18)***

I pray that this book has given you wisdom and revelation and has enlightened your understanding concerning the hope of your calling; so that you too can **ESCAPE FROM THE TRAP OF TRADITION!**

176

BIBLIOGRAPHY

Barnes Notes On The New Testament, Kregel Publications, Grand Rapids, MI.

The Gift Of The Apostle by David Cannistraci, Regal Books, Ventura, CA.

Moving In The Apostolic by John Eckhardt, Renew Books, Ventura, CA.

This Awakening Generation by John Osteen, Houston, TX.

Wycliffe Bible Encyclopedia, Moody Press, Chicago, IL.

The Hidden Power of Prayer and Fasting by Mahesh Chavda, Destiny Image Publishers, Shippensburg, PA

Prepare The Way by Robert Stearns, Creation House Publishers, Lake Mary, FL.

The Century Of The Holy Spirit by Vinson Synan, Thomas Nelson Publishers, Nashville, TN.

The Prophetic Flow by Apostle John Eckhardt, Crusaders Ministries, Chicago, IL.

Other Books Available by Apostle Williams

The Harry Potter book series claims to be innocent fantasy. ?????

Before you allow your children to be exposed to Harry Potter, learn the origin and facts surrounding the content of J.K. Rowling's featured character and **SEE HOW GOD VIEWS IT**.

In Witchcraft, The Occult & the Word of God, the second book to the answers of Harry Potter, one can see the difference between innocence and witchcraft or wizardry. Apostle Williams provides information based on the **Word of God** on how to test what spirit is behind a particular work.

God gave the children of Israel clear instruction not to practice divination and sorcery. God warns His people throughout scripture to totally forsake it all.

BLACK MAN COME HOME

A study manual that proves God's love for the BLACK MAN.

****

WHO SAID WOMEN CAN'T PREACH?

This book will challenge you to look again at those controversial scriptures where tradition has errored in its interpretation of what has been taught throughout the years. This book addresses the questions pertaining to make-up, wearing pants, adornment, and head coverings.

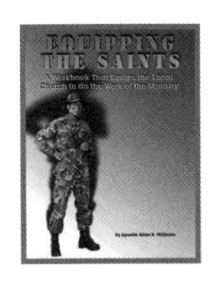

ATTENTION PASTORS!!

Are you ready to transition your church out of tradition but don't know where to begin?

Apostle Alton R. Williams has written a six volume workbook series of foundational teachings you must have to transition your church from tradition to truth. These lessons are all based upon sound, balanced biblical teachings.

These lessons can be used to train and equip your people to do the work of the ministry, to disciple your laity, for individual or group study as well as classroom lecture. Workbook topics include:

VOLUME 1 – TRADITION LIED TO ME ABOUT GOD

Where Do Tests and Trials Originate?
Is God Behind Accidents, Tragedies, Natural Disasters & Destruction in People Lives?
Who Is Behind Sickness & Death?
Is God Punishing Us?

VOLUME 2 – GETTING YOUR BASICS RIGHT
(Basic Biblical Doctrine)

Understanding Your Bible
Knowing Who God The Father Is
The Names Of God
Who Is Jesus?
Is the Holy Spirit God?
Do Christians Worship Three Gods?
Can I Trust The Scriptures?

VOLUME 3 – IT'S TIME TO WALK WITH GOD

What It Means To Be Born Again
Growing Up Spiritually
How To Be Right With God
Knowing Who You Are In Christ
God, I Need Some Power
Why Should I Speak In Tongues?
The Gifts Of The Spirit

VOLUME 4 – PRACTICING MY WALK WITH GOD

Can I Trust The Word Of God?
How To Believe God
Knowing What God Has Promised Me
How to Pray And Get Answers
What's All This Praise Business About?

VOLUME 5 – KNOWING WHAT BELONGS TO ME (Forgetting Not God's Benefits)

Is Healing For All?
Prosperity: You Mean God Wants Me to Prosper.

VOLUME 6 – THE SPIRIT WORLD AND THE AFTER LIFE

Satan And His Kingdom
Witchcraft & The Occult
The Ministry Of Angels
The Authority Of The Believer
Death, Afterlife, Future Events & End Times

Pastors, if you are ready to take your church to a new level of understanding, these workbooks are for you.

Understanding For Life Ministries

3665 Kirby Parkway
Suite 6
Memphis, TN 38115
(901) 844-3962 • Fax (901) 844-3944

Order Form

Name _____

Address _____

City _____ State _____ Zip _____

Phone _____

CODE	QTY	ITEM NAME	PRICE	TOTAL
EQST		Equipping The Saints Workbooks (Volumes 1-6)	$75.00	
WPRE		Who Said Women Can't Preach?	$12.00	
HP		Harry Potter Meets The Potter	$10.00	
HP		Harry Potter & Witchcraft	$12.00	
BLKMN		Black Man Come Home	$12.00	
		Shipping/Handling		
		Total Enclosed		

Shipping & Handling
Up to $5.00 $1.00
$5.01 to $50.00 $2.50
$50.01 to $100.00 $3.50
$101.00 to $150.00 $5.00
$150.01 to $200.00 $6.00
$200.00 and up $7.00

Payment Method:
[ ] Check
[ ] Money Order
[ ] Cashier's Check
[ ] Credit Card
    [ ] Visa   [ ] MC
    [ ] AMEX

Card # _____

Expiration Date _____

Signature: _____

NO CASH PLEASE
Thank you for your order.